MODERNIZING YOUR BRIDGE BIDDING

by

Gerald "Jerry" Olsen

DEDICATION

*I dedicate this book to
my secretary,
my best friend—
my wife, Helene.*

Published by Luminary Media Group, an imprint of Pine Orchard, Inc.
Visit us on the internet at www.pineorchard.com

Printed in Canada.

9 8 7 6 5 4 3 2 1

ISBN 1-930580-22-3

Library of Congress Control Number: 2001093870

Foreword from the Author

My experience with the game of Bridge is probably very similar to the people who will read and study this book. I started playing Bridge with friends in the 1960s. Although we only knew a few rudiments of the game, we enjoyed playing together. As I began to play with other people, I realized how little I knew about Bridge. My thirst for knowledge drove me to read about the game and study it in detail. Buying or borrowing books, studying in a library, and learning tips from more advanced players helped to quench that thirst.

Information from the American Contract Bridge League (ACBL) has helped me considerably. Limiting my playing to a few partners and studying with them have led to improvements in my game. Dwight Dorman, a master player, teacher, and director, offered invaluable help. We played much Duplicate Bridge together including sectional tournaments. Mr. Dorman also encouraged me to become a certified instructor and director so I could follow his role of teaching and directing on cruise ships.

Dave Bentley, my editor, made a second career in editing. I met him and his wife, Sue in one of my classes on board a cruise ship. The class was asking me to write a book. Dave volunteered to edit it. Having a friend and Bridge player as editor has helped me complete this book. Dave deserves considerable thanks for his editing of this book.

I now live in a community of senior citizens where I have been teaching and directing Duplicate Bridge. In 1993, I started teaching aboard various cruise ships. Most students in my community and on the ships are senior citizens.

Seniors play their hands well but often miss much joy of the game because they lack bidding skills. They learned their bidding in the 1950s, 1960s, and 1970s. Fantastic advancements have occurred in the last 30 years in bidding. As a student learns these techniques, I can see enjoyment glowing on their faces.

I wrote this from necessity. My students on cruise ships and at the country club where I live constantly asked me where they could obtain a book to study at home. I named three books. They wanted only one. They asked me to write a book. I did.

Table of Contents

1
INTRODUCTION AND ACKNOWLEDGMENTS

WHY DO PEOPLE PLAY THE GAME CALLED BRIDGE? Is it due to their innate competitive nature? Do they want to occupy leisure time? Are they searching for social pleasures? Is it to accommodate a spouse or friend?

All these items are benefits of playing Bridge. Another advantage that people rarely consider is mental health! A common adage states, "If you do not use it, you will lose it." This can apply to many things, but it is especially pertinent for the mind. An aging body needs exercise for all its parts including the brain.

Senior citizens who are playing Bridge today usually learned the game early in their lives. Many proven advances have occurred in the game since then. Today's players who adopt these changes can add considerable enjoyment to their Bridge playing and improve their scores. Younger adults who learned to play Bridge from these senior citizens can also benefit by learning the new concepts.

This book is not a beginner's Bridge book but a handbook for players who want to modernize their bidding process. The author therefore assumes that readers are already Bridge players who want to upgrade their bidding to a more advanced system. Readers should know the rudiments of the game including how to score and apply the bonus points for games, small slams, and grand slams.

Audrey Grant from the educational department of the American Contract Bridge League (ACBL) has conducted considerable research on Bridge. She has written a series of books using the results of her work. The format and much of the information in this book came from her books.

Ms. Grant's research showed new ways to evaluate a Bridge hand as a declarer and as a responder. After explaining these techniques, this book provides detailed information for opening bids in a suit and No Trump. Additional information on suit contracts discusses bids by the responder and rebids by opener and responder.

The chapters covering No Trump bidding include the Stayman and Jacoby Transfer conventions because they are often integral parts of such bids. The final chapters cover weak bids, strong bids, take-out doubles, and overcalls.

Each chapter except Chapter 11, "Other Bidding Conventions," in this book has a discussion, a summary, and a quiz. Answers to the quiz questions provide a brief explanation. This book is not only a good text for teachers but also an invaluable aid to individuals. These individuals should preferably study it with their intended Bridge partner.

Bridge players who always have the same partners and use the old systems for bidding will tax their minds and retard the aging process. Although this is good, they should stimulate their brain by learning and using new, proven concepts. Learn these as an individual or with a partner. Use this book as a text for study with many players. Regardless of the approach you take, you will find that the techniques proposed in the chapters of this book will improve your Bridge game, increase your scores, and contribute to your increased enjoyment of the game. Your primary reason for playing Bridge is undoubtedly the same as that of the author—enjoyment!

2
BIDDING CONCEPTS

ALWAYS REMEMBER when you play Bridge that the game requires a partnership. You are not playing as an individual but as a team with your partner across the table. To play their hands to best advantage, the partnership requires information. You need information about your partner's hand, and your partner needs information about your hand. Studying and playing with the same partner can dramatically improve the playing ability of a partnership. The bidding may eventually become so precise that you feel you have cheated. You are not cheating but simply applying the proper techniques of bidding.

Bidding is the legal way to communicate with your Bridge partner. After arranging your hand, you need to tell your partner the strength and shape of the cards that you hold. You want to tell the partner how many points you have and the length of your suits. By bidding properly, you want to reach a final contract that will give your side the maximum advantage and produce the greatest score.

The principles in this book are guides rather than inflexible rules. They are not substitutes for carefully listening to all the bidding, and they are not substitutes for using your thinking process and creativity to reach appropriate conclusions.

Hand Evaluation

Most Bridge players use the system for counting high card points developed by Charles Goren more than 50 years ago:

Ace   4 points
King   3 points
Queen 2 points
Jack   1 point

The initial point count today is different than that originally proposed by Goren. Shortages no longer have any value in an initial point count. Instead, long suits contribute the following points in an initial evaluation of a hand:

Five-card suit   1 point
Six-card suit   2 points
Seven-card suit   3 points
Eight-card suit   4 points

Before you feel betrayed by not counting shortages, be patient. Shortages do play a role in the system as you will see shortly. Research has proven that points for length are initially more valuable than shortage points. In many cases, points for length may be identical to points for shortages.

Adding all points for high cards to the points for length provides the total points to determine the worth of your hand for a possible opening bid. Consider the following examples that illustrate the proper way to count the points for high cards and the points for length in each suit:

Example 1

♠ A J 7
(5 high card points, 0 length points)

♥ K Q 9 7 6 2
(5 high card points, 2 length points)

♦ 10 9
(0 high card points, 0 length points)

♣ Q 7
(2 high card points, 0 length points)

Total: 14 points

Example 2

♠ K 7
(3 high card points, 0 length points)

♥ A 10 7 4 3
(4 high card points, 1 length point)

♦ Q J 7 6 2
(3 high card points, 1 length point)

♣ Q
(2 high card points, 0 length points)

Total: 14 points

Example 3

♠ A K 8 6 4

(7 high card points, 1 length point)

♥ A Q 9 7 2

(6 high card points, 1 length point)

♦ 10 2

(0 high card points, 0 length points)

♣ A

(4 high card points, 0 length points)

Total: 19 points

Opening the Bidding

The opening chapters of this book will consider bids and rebids by the opener (first bidder) and responder (his partner) without considering interference bidding. A later chapter will discuss takeout doubles and overcalls.

When your points from high cards plus your points from length total at least 13, you should make an opening bid. The specific bid will depend on the shape of your hand. Shape considers whether you have a balanced or unbalanced hand. A balanced hand must contain all the following features:

• No void
• No singleton
• No more than one doubleton.

An opening bid in No Trump requires a balanced hand. To open **1 NO TRUMP**, you must have 16–18 points with a balanced hand. An opening bid of **2 NO TRUMP** requires 20 or 21 points with a balanced hand. Most partnerships avoid bidding No Trump when their hands contain a major suit with five cards, but a previous partnership agreement is necessary.

Bidding an Opening Hand Containing a Suit with Five or More Cards

If a hand does not have the point value or shape to bid No Trump, you should bid a suit with a hand containing 13–21 points. If you have 2 five-card suits, bid the higher ranking suit—Spades over Hearts, Hearts over Diamonds, etc. If you have a six-card suit and a five-card suit with a minimum hand of 13–16 points, treat them as 2 five-card suits. Bid the higher ranking first. If you have an above average hand with 17 or 18 points, bid the six-card suit first. This technique will allow you to reverse if necessary.

A reverse is bidding a higher ranking suit at the 2 level than you had bid at the 1 level. If you had bid **1 DIAMOND**, for example, a subsequent bid of **2 HEARTS** is a reverse bid because Hearts rank higher than Diamonds. The bidder needs 17 or more points to make a reverse bid. A reverse bid is forcing. The partner must bid again.

Convenient Minors

With no suit containing five or more cards in an unbalanced hand that has 13–21 points, you must open in a minor suit. Use the following guides for convenient minor bids:

- Bid 1 of your longest suit.

- With two minor suits containing four cards each, bid **1 DIAMOND**.

- With two minor suits containing three cards each, bid **1 CLUB**.

Your hand may have only five cards in the minor suits with four Hearts and four Spades. Bid the longer minor suit.

Bidding with 22 or More Points

When your hand contains 22 or more points, your opening bid is **2 CLUBS**. This demand bid forces your partner to respond with a bid. Keep responding at least until the contract reaches game level.

Preemptive Bids

An opening bid of 3 in a suit or opening bids of **2 DIAMONDS**, **2 HEARTS**, or **2 SPADES** are preemptive bids. A later chapter will discuss using these bids.

Summary

Hand Evaluation

High card points		Distribution points	
Ace	= 4	Five-card suit	= 1
King	= 3	Six-card suit	= 2
Queen	= 2	Seven-card suit	= 3
Jack	= 1	Eight-card suit	= 4

Opening the Bidding

- With less than 13 points, pass.

- With 16–18 points and a balanced hand, bid **1 NO TRUMP**.

- With 20 or 21 points and a balanced hand, bid **2 NO TRUMP**.

- With 13–21 points and an unbalanced hand,

    with a five-card or longer suit:

    - Bid your longest suit.

    - Bid the higher ranking of 2 five-card or 2 six-card suits.

    with no five-card or longer suit:

    - Bid your longest minor suit.

    - Bid **1 DIAMOND** with 2 four-card minor suits.

    - Bid **1 CLUB** with 2 three-card minor suits.

- With 22 or more points, bid **2 CLUBS**.

Quiz

For each of the following hands, determine the number of points and the proper opening bid.

1.

♠ A K 10 7 5
♥ J 6 2
♦ A 9 2
♣ 8 4

2.

♠ K 9 5 2
♥ A J 9 4
♦ Q 9 2
♣ K 4

3.

♠ K 2
♥ A 10 5
♦ Q J 10 6
♣ K 7 5 3

4.

♠ K Q 4
♥ A 10 8 2
♦ Q J 7
♣ K 9 3

5.

♠ A K J 4
♥ 8 7 6 5 4
♦ A 6
♣ Q 10

6.

♠ 10 9 8 6 5 3
♥ A K Q
♦ 9 8
♣ Q J

7.

♠ A Q J
♥ 9 6 4 3 2
♦ J 9 4 3
♣ 9

8.

♠ 8 6 3
♥ A Q J 9
♦ K 9 8
♣ A K Q

9.
- ♠ K J 7 3
- ♥ A 9 5
- ♦ Q J 6
- ♣ A J 10

10.
- ♠ J 7
- ♥ K 9 4 3
- ♦ K Q 10 5
- ♣ A J 8

11.
- ♠ K Q 3
- ♥ A
- ♦ Q 8 6 4 2
- ♣ K J 6 5

12.
- ♠ K 8
- ♥ A K 8 6 2
- ♦ K Q 7 3
- ♣ 9 5

13.
- ♠ K 8
- ♥ 9 5 2
- ♦ A Q 8
- ♣ K Q J 7 3

14.
- ♠ Q 6
- ♥ K 4 2
- ♦ A J 8 7 5 2
- ♣ K 3

15.
- ♠ 9 6 4
- ♥ Q J 9 8
- ♦ A K 4
- ♣ A Q J

16.
- ♠ A J 9 8 7
- ♥ K 7
- ♦ K J 8 2
- ♣ 9 8

17.
- ♠ 10 9 8
- ♥ Q 9 8 7 6
- ♦ A Q J
- ♣ 8 5

18.
- ♠ 3
- ♥ A J 8 6 5
- ♦ K 4
- ♣ A K J 7 3

19.

♠ A Q 7 3
♥ A 9 5
♦ 7 6
♣ K J 6 2

20.

♠ A J 6 3
♥ 5
♦ K J 9 4
♣ A 8 6 2

21.

♠ K 4 3
♥ A K 8 6
♦ A Q 5
♣ K J 2

22.

♠ Q 8 5 3
♥ Q 9 6 3
♦ A J 10
♣ A 6

23.

♠ 4
♥ A Q J 6 3
♦ 5
♣ A K 10 7 5 2

24.

♠ A Q 3 2
♥ K 4 3
♦ 9
♣ A Q 8 7 2

25.

♠ 10 9 8 5 4
♥ A Q J 9
♦ K 7
♣ Q 2

Answers

1. 12 points for high cards and 1 point for length = 13 points; bid **1 SPADE**.

2. 13 points for high cards with no five-card major; bid **1 DIAMOND** (the longest minor).

3. 13 points for high cards with 2 four-card minors; bid **1 DIAMOND**. (Your next bid can be Clubs.)

4. 15 points for high cards with no five-card major and 2 three-card minor suits; bid **1 CLUB**.

5. 14 points for high cards and 1 point for length = 15 points; bid **1 HEART**. (Length in the trump suit is the important factor. Your partner may have A K Q.)

6. 12 points for high cards and 2 points for length = 14 points; bid **1 SPADE**. (Depending on the response from your partner, you may bid Spades again since you hold six Spades.)

7. 8 points for high cards and 1 point for length = 9 points; pass.

8. 19 points for high cards; bid **1 CLUB**. (This hand is too strong for **1 NO TRUMP**, although it does have balance. You may jump shift on your next bid to show the strength.)

9. 16 points for high cards with balance; bid **1 NO TRUMP**.

10. 14 points for high cards; bid **1 DIAMOND**.

11. 15 points for high cards and 1 point for length = 16 points without balance; bid **1 DIAMOND**.

12. 15 points for high cards and 1 point for length = 16 points without balance; bid **1 HEART**.

13. 15 points for high cards and 1 point for length = 16 points; bid **1 CLUB** since only high card points count for No Trump bids.

14. 13 points for high cards and 2 points for length = 15 points; bid **1 DIAMOND**. (You may want to bid the same suit again at your next turn.)

15. 17 points for high cards with balance; bid **1 NO TRUMP**.

16. 12 points for high cards and 1 point for length = 13 points; bid **1 SPADE**.

17. 9 points for high cards and 1 point for length = 10 points; pass.

18. 16 points for high cards and 2 points for length = 18 points without balance; bid **1 HEART**. (Bid the higher ranking of 2 five-card suits. You might bid Clubs at your next turn if your partner does not bid Hearts.)

19. 14 points for high cards; bid **1 CLUB**.

20. 13 points for high cards; bid **1 DIAMOND**.

21. 20 points for high cards with balance; bid **2 NO TRUMP**.

22. 13 points for high cards; bid **1 DIAMOND**.

23. 14 points for high cards and 3 points for length = 17 points without balance; bid **1 CLUB**. (With 17 points, you can afford to reverse. After bidding **1 CLUB**, bid Hearts twice if bidding permits.)

24. 15 points for high cards and 1 point for length = 16 points without balance; bid **1 CLUB**.

25. 12 points for high cards and 1 point for length = 13 points; bid **1 SPADE**.

3
RESPONSES TO OPENING BIDS OF ONE IN A SUIT

AFTER THE FIRST MEMBER of a partnership makes an opening bid, the partner must respond. The person making the opening bid has revealed information about his hand. Now, the partner must provide some information about his cards by his response.

This chapter will only describe responses to opening bids of 1 in a suit. Subsequent chapters will cover responses to opening bids of **1 NO TRUMP**, strong bids of **2 CLUBS** or **2 NO TRUMP**, and weak bids of **2 DIAMONDS**, **2 HEARTS**, or **2 SPADES**.

Responding to an Opening Bid of One in a Major Suit

An opening bid of **1 HEART** or **1 SPADE** indicates at least 13 points with at least five cards in that suit. The responder must now start to describe his hand. With less than 6 points, the responder should pass.

Counting Shortages

The discussion in the previous chapter mentioned that shortage points can be important when evaluating a hand. This occurs when you are the responder to the opening bidder. Count the shortages in your hand when you have at least three cards in your partner's major suit and you and your partner have a fit. A fit is a total of eight or more cards in the major suit between the two hands.

With a fit in a major suit, the responder should re-evaluate his hand using shortage points rather than points for length. Such additions do require using common sense. The responder may add the following points to his hand value:

Void   = up to 5 points
Singleton   = up to 3 points
Doubleton   = 1 point

Notice the use of the term "up to." Common sense would probably dictate that a singleton Ace is not worth 7 points (4 points for the Ace and 3 points for the singleton). Similarly, a singleton Queen is not worth 5 points (2 points for the Queen and 3 points for the singleton). Note that a singleton Ace in the opponent's suit could be worth 7 points.

Be certain your partnership has a fit before you start adding shortage points. Do not add shortage points in a minor suit or No Trump. Note that shortages are a negative feature for a No Trump hand. Initial minor suit bids could eventually lead to a final contract in No Trump.

Players should add shortage points to the hand that may become the dummy hand. This is not always the hand of the responder. For example, opener could bid

1 HEART followed by responder's bid of **1 SPADE**. In this case, assume the opener has four Spades. Since the opener's hand now has the potential to be the dummy hand, he can count shortage points.

Responding with 6–9 Points

With 6–9 points and at least three cards in the partner's major suit, responder can bid 2 in the suit. Holding 6–9 points without three cards in the opener's suit, bid a new suit at the 1 level or bid **1 NO TRUMP**. For the **1 NO TRUMP** bid, you do not need stoppers in the unbid suits unless the opponents have bid that suit.

Always remember that a new suit bid by the responder requires the opener to bid again. This rule has no exceptions.

Responding with 10–12 Points

With 10–12 points, the responder should make a forcing bid. This is a bid by the responder in any new suit regardless of the level. Most jump bids are also forcing as discussed later.

With 10–12 points, bid a new suit at the 1 or 2 level even when you have support for your partner's major suit. If you bid a new suit at the 2 level, your partner knows you have at least 10 points. You will bid your partner's major suit later if you have support with three or more cards.

An exception occurs when responder has 11 or 12 points and a four-card support for the partner's suit. Jump to the 3 level in the opener's suit. This is a limit raise. It means the responder has exactly 11 or 12 points and four-card support. You may count shortage points.

Responding with 13 or More Points

With 13 or more points and support in opener's major suit, bid a new suit at the 1 or 2 level. This forcing bid requires the opener to continue bidding until reaching a game contract. Bid **2 NO TRUMP** with a balanced hand and no five-card suit.

If you have at least three cards in the opener's major suit, you can bid to game later.

Responding to an Opening Bid of One in a Minor Suit

With less than 6 points, the responder should pass.

Responding with 6–9 Points

If the opener has bid a minor suit, bid a five-card suit or the higher ranking of 2 five-card suits at the 1 level. If you do not have a five-card suit, bid a new four-card suit at the 1 level. If you have more than 1 four-card suit, bid the lower ranking suit even if that suit is Diamonds. This is bidding up the line—bidding four-card suits from lower to higher ranking. Bid this way even when you have a very strong hand.

Advantages of bidding four-card suits up the line are the following:

- You provide considerable information at the 1 level.

- When you bid Diamonds over Clubs, opener has a chance to name his four-card major suit. You also tell opener you have a Diamond suit if he wishes to bid No Trump.

- If opener names his major suit and responder has four cards, your partnership has a fit. The weak hand will be the dummy.

- When a fit occurs in a major suit, the responder to that bid can count shortage points.

With 6–9 points and no four-card major suit, responder can bid 2 in the opener's minor suit with five-card support. Otherwise, bid **1 NO TRUMP**. When responder raises the opener's bid to the 2 level or bids **1 NO TRUMP**, he indicates that his hand only has 6–9 points. This is another example of a limiting bid. *Do not confuse limit raises with limiting bids.*

Responding with 10–12 Points

Bid a new suit. This should be your five-card suit or the higher ranking of 2 five-card suits. With no five-card suit to bid, bid four-card suits up the line.

If partner has opened **1 DIAMOND** and you have no four-card major, you can respond **2 CLUBS**. This indicates at least 10 points. Avoid responding **1 NO TRUMP**. That would be a limiting bid showing 6–9 points.

Responding with 13 or More Points

Respond with a forcing bid as you would with 10–12 points but consider the following additions if they apply:

- With a balanced hand and no four-card or longer major suit, jump to **2 NO TRUMP**.

- With five cards in opener's minor, jump to the 3 level in his suit.

Note that a responder should always bid a four-card major suit even if it is weak. If you do not bid the four-card major suit, you deny that you have it.

Summary

Responses to Opening Bids
of One in a Suit

0–5 points:

Pass.

6–9 points:

When responding to a major suit:

- Raise to the 2 level with three-card or longer support.

- Bid a new suit at the 1 level.

- Bid **1 NO TRUMP.**

When responding to a minor suit:

- Raise to the 2 level with five-card or longer support.

- Bid the higher ranking of 2 five-card suits.

- Bid a new four-card suit at the 1 level. (With more than 1 four-card suit, bid the lower ranking suit and bid up the line in subsequent bids.)

- Bid **1 NO TRUMP.**

10–12 points:

When responding to a major suit:
- Bid a new suit at the 1 or 2 level.

- With 11–12 points and four-card support, jump to the 3 level.

When responding to a minor suit:

- Bid a new five-card suit or the higher ranking of 2 five-card suits.

- Bid four-card suits up the line.

- With no four-card major suit, bid a four-card Club suit when partner opens **1 DIAMOND**.

13 or more points:

When responding to a major suit:

- Bid a new suit at the 1 or 2 level with support in opener's major suit.
- Bid **2 NO TRUMP** with a balanced hand and no five-card suit.

When responding to a minor suit:

- Bid as with 10–12 points except consider the following:
  - Bid **2 NO TRUMP** with a balanced hand and no five-card suit.
  - Raise to the 3 level with five-card or longer support.

Quiz

You hold the following hands. Your partner has opened the bidding with **1 HEART**. What is the point value of your hand? What is your responding bid?

1.

♠ 7 4
♥ J 7 5 4
♦ K Q 7
♣ A 9 8 3

2.

♠ K 3 2
♥ J 9 8 2
♦ J 10 8
♣ A 6 2

3.

♠ J 9 7 3
♥ Q 7
♦ A 6 4 3 2
♣ 10 6

4.

♠ 10 9 7 3
♥ Q J
♦ A 7 3
♣ J 10 6 3

5.

♠ 7 5 4
♥ K 6
♦ Q J 9 8 6 4
♣ J 8

You hold the following hands. Your partner has opened the bidding with **1 CLUB**. What is the point value of your hand? What is your responding bid?

6.

♠ 9 8 6 5
♥ Q 10 8 6 3
♦ K 3
♣ Q 6

7.

♠ 8 5
♥ Q J 7
♦ J 9 3
♣ K 10 8 7 3

8.

♠ K 9 3
♥ Q 10 8
♦ A J 2
♣ 7 5 4 2

9.

♠ K 7 6 3
♥ 8 5
♦ Q 7 6 5 3
♣ A 2

10.

♠ K 7 6
♥ Q 8 2
♦ J 5
♣ Q 9 6 4 2

You hold the following hands. Your partner has opened the bidding with **1 DIAMOND**. What is the point value of your hand? What is your responding bid?

11.

♠ A Q 8 7
♥ K 3
♦ K J 9 5 2
♣ 7 5

12.

♠ A J 10
♥ K J 9
♦ K 10 7 3
♣ Q 9 6

13.

♠ 9 8 4 2
♥ Q 8 7
♦ K J 4 3
♣ J 3

14.

♠ J 10
♥ J 4 3
♦ Q 9 8
♣ K 9 7 5 3

15.

♠ 9 5 3
♥ Q J 10 8 7
♦ Q 6
♣ J 5 3

You hold the following hands. Your partner has opened the bidding with **1 SPADE**. What is the point value of your hand? What is your responding bid?

16.
- ♠ 9 8 7 3
- ♥ K 6
- ♦ Q J 10 4
- ♣ A 9 4

17.
- ♠ 7 3
- ♥ A Q 9 8 3
- ♦ J 6 3
- ♣ K J 10

18.
- ♠ 8
- ♥ J 6 3
- ♦ Q J 10 8 6
- ♣ A Q J 9

19.
- ♠ A Q 8 3
- ♥ A 5
- ♦ Q J 10 6
- ♣ 7 6 4

20.
- ♠ J 7
- ♥ K Q 10
- ♦ A J 8 4
- ♣ K J 6 4

Answers

1. With the fit in hearts, count shortages: 10 points for high cards and 1 point for the shortage in Spades = 11 points; bid **3 HEARTS** (a limit raise).

2. 9 points for high cards and 0 points for shortages; bid **2 HEARTS**.

3. 7 points for high cards; bid **1 SPADE**. (Never bypass a four-card major even if it is weak.)

4. 8 points for high cards; bid **1 SPADE**. (Same as number 3.)

5. 7 points for high cards; bid **1 NO TRUMP**. (You would need 10 or more points to bid **2 DIAMONDS**.)

6. 7 points for high cards; bid **1 HEART**.

7. 7 points for high cards; bid **2 CLUBS**. (The hand has no four-card suit higher than clubs. Do not count shortage points in minor suits because you may be playing the hand in No Trump. Shortages are negative features for No Trump bids. The Spade suit is too weak for No Trump.)

8. 10 points for high cards; bid **2 DIAMONDS**. (The hand has no new suit to bid at the 1 level. The bid of **2 DIAMONDS** shows 10 points and is forcing. You should plan to bid No Trump next. A bid of **1 NO TRUMP** would have shown only 6–9 points.)

9. 9 points for high cards; bid **1 DIAMOND**. (Bid up the line. If opener rebids Hearts, you then bid Spades.)

10. 8 points for high cards; bid **1 NO TRUMP**. (The honor card in each of the unbid suits makes the No Trump bid slightly preferable over **2 CLUBS**.)

11. 13 points for high cards; bid **1 SPADE**. (This is a forcing bid. If you do not bid the Spade, you are denying it.)

12. 14 points for high cards; bid **2 NO TRUMP**. (You have no four-card major.)

13. 7 points for high cards; bid **1 SPADE**. (Do not deny a four-card major. Your partner may have A K Q J.)

14. 7 points for high cards; bid **1 NO TRUMP**. (You have no four-card major.)

15. 6 points for high cards; bid **1 HEART**. (This is your five-card major.)

16. 10 points for high cards; bid **2 DIAMONDS**. (Although the hand fits with the opening partner, assigning 4 points to K 7 is stretching the value of the hand. Bidding **2 DIAMONDS** as a forcing bid is better than **3 SPADES**, a limit raise.)

17. 11 points for high cards; bid **2 HEARTS**. (This is a forcing bid that shows 10 or more points.)

18. 11 points for high cards; bid **2 DIAMONDS**. (This is a forcing bid. You may want to bid Clubs or No Trump if opener bids Hearts.)

19. 13 points for high cards; bid **2 DIAMONDS**. (Although the hands fit, adding points for A 7 is stretching the value of the hand. With the forcing bid of **2 DIAMONDS**, you can bid game in Spades at your next bid.)

20. 15 points for high cards; bid **2 NO TRUMP**.

4
REBIDS BY OPENER

THE QUEST NOW CONTINUES to communicate legally the strength and shape of the hands of the partnership to reach an optimum contract. The opener must make a second bid that accomplishes one of the following:

- Reveals strength of his hand.
- Provides better description of the shape of his hand.
- Gives information on both previous factors.
- Sets the final contract.

The following are guidelines the opener should use to convey his strength:

13–16 points	Minimum hand
17–18 points	Above-average hand
19–21 points	Maximum hand

Note that the maximum hand can only be 21 points. If the opener had more than 21 points, he would have opened with **2 CLUBS**.

Opener's Rebid After Responder Raises Opener's Bid in a Major Suit

If opener had bid a major suit and responder had raised the major suit to the 2 level, opener's rebid would be as follows:

- Minimum hand: Pass.
- Above-average hand: Raise to 3 level.
- Maximum hand: Jump to game.

The logic for these bids is that the partnership must have 26 points total in both hands to make a major suit bid of game. When responder raised to the 2 level in opener's major suit, he limited his hand to 6–9 points.

If opener has an above-average hand after responder raises his major suit to the 2 level, he should raise to the 3 level in that suit. The responder now knows that the opener has 17–18 points. If the responder has 8 or 9 points, he can feel reasonably certain of sufficient strength to make game. If opener has 17 points and responder has 8 points, the total is only 25 points. This point level might be a good gamble.

If responder has raised the major suit to the 2 level and the opener has a maximum hand, he should immediately jump to game.

The situation is different if responder raises the opener's major suit to the 3 level. Remember this is a limit raise showing exactly 11 or 12 points and four-card support. Some deductive reasoning is necessary. If opener has only 13 points and a balanced hand, he should pass. If opener has 13 or 14 points with a decent second suit and a shortage or two, he may well decide to bid game. The shape of his hand should be a factor. With 14–18 points, opener should bid game. If opener has a maximum hand, he should explore slam with cue bids—

Blackwood or Key Card Blackwood—after a limit raise. (The final chapter discusses these conventions.)

Opener's Rebid After Responder Bids a New Suit at the 1 Level

When responder bids a new suit at the 1 level, he has made a forcing bid. Opener must rebid.

With Minimum Hand of 13–16 Points

If opener has opened with a six-card major suit, he should rebid that suit. Responder then knows opener has six cards. Responder then only needs two cards in the suit for a fit. With that fit, he can count shortage points because his hand is potentially the dummy.

If responder has bid a major suit and opener has four cards in that suit, opener should raise to the 2 level. With no major suit fit with responder, opener can now bid a second suit at the 1 level. With 2 four-card suits at the 1 level, bid the lower ranking first—bidding up the line. If opener does not have a new four-card suit at the 1 level, he can bid a new suit at the 2 level if it is not a higher ranking suit than he had bid at the 1 level to avoid a reverse bid. With a balanced hand and stoppers in all suits not yet bid, opener can bid **1 NO TRUMP**. With a five-card or longer minor suit, opener can also bid that suit. When responding, opener should never ignore a four-card major in the bidding process.

As stated in Chapter 2, a reverse bid is bidding a new suit at the 2 level that ranks higher than the initial suit bid at the 1 level. The point requirement is at least 17 points. A reverse bid is forcing.

With Above-Average Hand of 17 or 18 Points

With an above-average hand and a six-card or longer major, opener should jump one level in his major suit. Responder then knows opener has at least a six-card major suit with 17 or 18 points. If responder has two cards in opener's major suit, the partnership has a fit. Responder can count shortage points. With 8 or more points, responder can then bid game. With 13 points or more, responder may consider trying a slam bid.

With four-card support in responder's major, opener should jump one level. If responder had bid a major suit at the 1 level, opener should bid 3 of that suit. Responder needed four or more cards for his bid. Opener has a four-card suit. This indicates a fit. Opener can now count shortage points because he potentially holds the dummy hand.

Opener can also bid a second suit of four cards with a strong hand. This new suit bid is forcing. Responder must bid again. Opener can bid a four-card or longer suit at the 2 level even if it is a higher ranking suit from his first bid at the 1 level. This is the reverse bid described above.

With Maximum Hand of 19–21 Points

When responder bids a major suit and opener has four cards in support, opener can jump two levels. Opener can count shortage points because he potentially holds the dummy hand.

Opener can bid a second four-card suit jumping one level. This is a jump shift telling responder he has 19–21 points. Opener can also jump shift to No Trump if he has a balanced hand and stoppers in unbid suits.

When responder bids opener's major suit at the 2 level, opener can jump to game.

Opener's Rebid After Responder Bids a New Suit at the 2 Level

When responder has bid a new suit at the 2 level, opener knows his partner has at least 10 points. This is a forcing bid so opener must bid again. He must give a bid to tell responder the strength of his hand.

With Minimum Hand of 13–16 Points

With 13 or 14 points, opener should keep the bidding open. He may rebid his original major suit with six-card support or rebid a five-card minor. With a fit in responder's major suit bid, opener should raise to the 3 level.

Holding 15 or 16 points, opener should pursue game. With 15 or 16 points and a fit in partner's major suit, opener can bid game in that suit.

Remember that a bid by opener in a new suit would force responder to bid again. If opener wants to bid No Trump, he may bid at the 2 level with 13 or 14 points or the 3 level with 15 or 16 points.

With Above-Average Hand of 17 or 18 Points

With an above-average hand, opener knows the final contract will be at least the game level but might be slam. Opener may have sufficient information to jump to game, or he may want to keep the bidding open by bidding a new suit. Any bid except **7 NO TRUMP** indicates to the responder that the opener wants to continue bidding.

With Maximum Hand of 19–21 Points

Bidding to slam level is a definite possibility. Opener should relay that information to responder. By bidding at the 2 level, responder has stated he has 10 points minimum. Opener does not know how many more points are in responder's hand.

If opener makes a forcing bid, he gives the responder an opportunity to show the strength in that hand. Simultaneously, the bid by the opener describes his hand in more detail. If a fit exists and shortage points provide extra value, Blackwood bidding may be useful. Be careful not to miss a slam bid.

Opener's Rebid After Responder Raises in a Minor Suit

Responder shows 6–9 points and five cards in the suit when he raises opener's bid. Opener should pass with a minimum hand. Holding an above-average hand, opener can raise to the 3 level. If opener has a maximum hand, he should normally jump to **3 NO TRUMP**. With a hand containing many points in shortages, opener may be able to bid 5 in the minor suit. When responder had bid 2 in the minor suit, the partnership had a fit. Opener could therefore count shortages. The opener's hand could conceivably be re-evaluated to 23 or more points, and he could bid at the 5 level in the minor suit.

Opener's Rebid After Responder Bids 1 NO TRUMP

With Minimum Hand of 13–16 Points

With a minimum hand, opener can bid his major suit at the 2 level if his hand contains six or more cards in that suit. With a minimum hand that is balanced, opener could pass so the partnership would play **1 NO TRUMP**.

Opener could bid a new four-card or longer suit at the 2 level if it is lower ranking than his original bid. This is not a reverse bid.

With Above-Average Hand of 17–18 Points

Opener with an above-average hand can jump to the 3 level with six or more cards in his opening major bid.

Responder would need only two cards in the suit to have a fit. If he could re-evaluate his hand using shortage points to 8 or more points, he could bid game.

Another bid for opener would be a four-card suit at the 2 level even if it is higher ranking than the original bid at the 1 level. The new suit shows extra strength, and responder should bid again.

With Maximum Hand of 19–21 Points

With a balanced, maximum hand, opener can jump to game in No Trump. Opener can jump shift to a four-card or longer suit if it is a lower ranking than his original bid. If it is higher ranking, bid it at the 2 level. Both these bids are forcing, and responder must bid again. With six cards or longer in his original bid of a major suit, opener can jump to game in the major suit.

Summary

Opener's Rebid After Responder Raises a Major Suit

13–16 points (minimum hand):
Pass.

17–18 points (above-average hand):
Raise to the 3 level.

19–21 points (maximum hand):
Jump raise to the 4 level (game).

Opener's Rebid After Responder Bids a New Suit

13–16 points (minimum hand):
Rebid a six-card major.

- Raise partner's major to the lowest available level with four-card support (count shortage points).

- Bid a second suit of a four-card or longer suit at the 1 level or bid a new suit at the 2 level if it is a lower ranking suit from your first bid.

- Bid No Trump with a balanced hand at the lowest available level.

- As a last resort, rebid a five-card major suit.

17–18 points (above-average hand):
- Raise partner's major suit by jumping one level with four-card support (count shortage points).

- Bid a second suit of four-card or longer even if it is higher-ranking than the original and must be bid at the 2 level.

19–21 points (maximum hand):
- Raise partner's major suit by jumping two levels with four-card support (count shortage points).

- Bid a second suit of four-card or longer by jumping one level (jump shift).

- Bid No Trump with a balanced hand by jumping one level.

- Rebid the original suit by jumping to game with six cards.

Opener's Rebid After Responder Bids a New Suit at the 2 Level

13–14 points (minimum hand):
- Rebid original major suit with six-card support.

- Rebid a five-card minor suit.

- Bid **2 NO TRUMP.**

15–16 points (minimum hand):
- With a fit in partner's major suit, bid game in that suit.

- Bid **3 NO TRUMP.**

17–18 points (above-average hand):
- Keep the bidding open by bidding a new suit.

- Jump to game.

19–21 points (maximum hand):
Explore bidding to slam level.

Opener's Rebid After Responder
Raises a Minor Suit

13–16 points (minimum hand):
Pass.

17–18 points (above-average hand):
Raise to the 3 level.

19–21 points (maximum hand):
- Jump to **3 NO TRUMP**.

- Bid 5 in a minor suit if re-evaluation shows 23 or more points.

Opener's Rebid After Responder
Bids **1 NO TRUMP**

13–16 points (minimum hand):
- Pass with a balanced hand.

- Bid a second suit of four cards or longer if it is lower ranking than the original suit bid at the 1 level.

- Rebid the original major suit at the 2 level with six or more cards.

17–18 points (above-average hand):
- Bid a second suit of four cards or longer even if it is higher ranking than the original suit.

- Rebid the original major suit with six or more cards at the lowest level.

19–21 points (maximum hand):

- Bid **3 NO TRUMP** with a balanced hand.

- Bid a second suit of four cards or longer by jumping a level (jump shift) if it is lower ranking than the original suit.

- Rebid the original suit by jumping to game with a good six- or seven-card suit.

Quiz

In each of the following hands, you hold the indicated cards. You are the opening bidder and have made the indicated bid. Your partner has made a response. What is your rebid?

1.

♠ A K 10 9 8 2
♥ J 10 9
♦ 5 3
♣ K 3

OPENING BID: **1 SPADE**
RESPONSE: **2 SPADES**

2.

♠ A Q J 7 4 2
♥ A 9
♦ 7 4 2
♣ A 6

OPENING BID: **1 SPADE**
RESPONSE: **2 SPADES**

3.

♠ K Q 10 7 6 2
♥ Q 4
♦ A K
♣ A J 8

OPENING BID: **1 SPADE**
RESPONSE: **2 SPADES**

4.

♠ K 9 5
♥ K J 7 5 3
♦ A 8 2
♣ J 7

OPENING BID: **1 HEART**
RESPONSE: **2 HEARTS**

5.
♠ 10 6
♥ A Q 10 6 5 3
♦ A Q J 8
♣ 5
OPENING BID: **1 HEART**
RESPONSE: **2 HEARTS**

6.
♠ Q 9 7
♥ J 10
♦ A 9 8 7 6 3
♣ K Q
OPENING BID: **1 DIAMOND**
RESPONSE: **2 DIAMONDS**

7.
♠ 9 8
♥ A K 6
♦ K Q J 6 4 2
♣ J 9
OPENING BID: **1 DIAMOND**
RESPONSE: **2 DIAMOND**

8.
♠ A Q 7
♥ K 10
♦ K J 10 7 4
♣ K Q 9
OPENING BID: **1 DIAMOND**
RESPONSE: **2 DIAMONDS**

9.
♠ K 7 3
♥ A Q 10 9 5
♦ K 10 3
♣ 8 2
OPENING BID: **1 HEART**
RESPONSE: **1 NO TRUMP**

10.
♠ 9 6 2
♥ A K 10 8 6 2
♦ A J 4
♣ 6
OPENING BID: **1 HEART**
RESPONSE: **1 NO TRUMP**

11.
♠ 4
♥ K J 5
♦ K Q 10 6 3
♣ A Q J 8
OPENING BID: **1 DIAMOND**
RESPONSE: **1 NO TRUMP**

12.
♠ K Q J 9 7 6 3
♥ 5
♦ A J
♣ A Q J
OPENING BID: **1 SPADE**
RESPONSE: **1 NO TRUMP**

13.

♠ A K J 7 5 3
♥ K Q
♦ A Q 8
♣ 5 3

OPENING BID: **1 SPADE**
RESPONSE: **2 SPADES**

14.

♠ K Q 10 9 6 2
♥ 5 4
♦ K Q 8
♣ A J

OPENING BID: **1 SPADE**
RESPONSE: **2 SPADES**

15.

♠ A Q 8 5
♥ K 10 6 3
♦ J 9
♣ Q J 2

OPENING BID: **1 CLUB**
RESPONSE: **2 CLUBS**

16.

♠ A J 10
♥ K J
♦ 9 7 3
♣ A K Q J 8

OPENING BID: **1 CLUB**
RESPONSE: **2 CLUBS**

17.

♠ 9 3
♥ A
♦ A 10 8 7 3
♣ K Q 6 4 3

OPENING BID: **1 DIAMOND**
RESPONSE: **1 NO TRUMP**

18.

♠ A 5
♥ K J 9
♦ A K J 7 3
♣ A 5 2

OPENING BID: **1 DIAMOND**
RESPONSE: **1 NO TRUMP**

19.

♠ A Q 3
♥ J 8 7
♦ A K Q 10 6 3
♣ 6

OPENING BID: **1 DIAMOND**
RESPONSE: **1 NO TRUMP**

20.

♠ Q J 10 9
♥ A 3
♦ K Q 9 7 6 4
♣ 9

OPENING BID: **1 DIAMOND**
RESPONSE: **1 NO TRUMP**

21.

♠ A 9 3
♥ K 7 6 4
♦ A Q 7 3 2
♣ 9

OPENING BID: **1 DIAMOND**
RESPONSE: **1 HEART**

22.

♠ A Q
♥ A K J 8 2
♦ K Q 10 6 3
♣ 5

OPENING BID: **1 HEART**
RESPONSE: **1 SPADE**

23.

♠ A 4
♥ A Q J 9 7 5 3
♦ K 3
♣ K 2

OPENING BID: **1 HEART**
RESPONSE: **1 SPADE**

24.

♠ A J 9 7 4
♥ A J
♦ K Q 6
♣ Q j 10

OPENING BID: **1 SPADE**
RESPONSE: **2 HEARTS**

25.

♠ A J 7 6 3
♥ K 9 5
♦ 8 4 2
♣ A 3

OPENING BID: **1 SPADE**
RESPONSE: **2 NO TRUMP**

Answers

1. 11 points for high cards, 2 points for length, and 1 point for shortage = 14 points; responder shows a minimum hand so the partnership does not have sufficient points for game; pass.

2. 17 points; above-average hand; responder's minimum hand makes game with 9 points; bid **3 SPADES**.

3. 21 points; maximum hand; bid game at **4 SPADES**.

4. The partnership has two minimum hands; pass.

5. With length and shortage points, the value of the hand is 18; bid **3 HEARTS**.

6. 14 points; partnership has two minimum hands; pass.

7. 15 points and 2 points for shortage; above-average hand; bid **3 DIAMONDS**.

8. 19 points; maximum hand; bid **3 NO TRUMP**.

9. 13 points; Club suit may be a problem; partnership has two minimum hands; pass.

10. Partnership has two minimum hands; rebid your six-card major suit.

11. 17 points; above-average hand; give responder a choice by bidding **2 CLUBS**. (Partner will probably pass or bid **3 DIAMONDS**.)

12. Maximum hand with seven-card suit; jump to game by bidding **4 SPADES**.

13. Maximum hand with a fit; responder has limited his hand; bid **4 SPADES**.

14. 18 points including 1 point for shortage; bid **3 SPADES** to show your above-average hand.

15. Partnership has two minimum hands; pass.

16. Maximum hand; bid **3 NO TRUMP**. (You may have a problem in Diamonds. Responder's points must be somewhere.)

17. Two minimum hands; give your partner a choice. (He states that he does not have a four-card major suit. He must therefore have some cards in the minor suits. Bid **2 CLUBS**.)

18. Maximum hand with stoppers; bid **3 NO TRUMP**.

19. 21 points; count shortage points because the hand will be played in Diamonds and the singleton is very valuable. Bid **4 DIAMONDS**. (If partner has 8 or 9 points, he will rebid **5 DIAMONDS**.)

20. Two minimum hands; rebid the Diamond suit at the 2 level.

21. 17 points; count shortages because your hand will be on the table; show an above-average hand by bidding **3 HEARTS**.

22. Maximum hand; jump shift by bidding **3 DIAMONDS**. (If partner has a Club suit, he can bid **3 NO TRUMP**.)

23. Maximum hand with seven trump cards; bid **4 HEARTS**. (Since partner has not limited his hand, a slam may be possible.)

24. 19 points; partner has at least 10 points; bid **3 NO TRUMP**. (A slam may be possible.)

25. Responder is showing at least an opening hand; bid **3 NO TRUMP**.

5
REBIDS BY RESPONDER

THE BIDDING PROCESS IS SIMILAR to a game of Ping-Pong or tennis where the ball passes from one person to the opposite player. In Bridge, the bid goes from one player in a partnership to the opposite person. In this chapter, the bid has now passed back to the responder. The opener has made two bids with one bid by responder interspersed between them. The responder therefore knows considerable information about the shape of the opener's hand. Still, the responder may want to ask the opener for additional information.

The opener might have told the responder the strength of his hand. If the opener rebids **1 NO TRUMP** and subsequently raised his own suit or the responder's suit at the 1 level, he has limited his hand to a minimum bid. If opener made a reverse bid or jumped in a suit already bid, he has shown an above-average hand. Jumping to game in a suit already bid, jumping to **3 NO TRUMP**, or making a Blackwood bid or a jump shift would indicate a maximum hand. Bidding a new suit at the 1 level or a new suit lower ranking from his original bid is a forcing bid. The opener did not show extra values by those bids. Instead, he was asking for more information.

In situations where the opener has given information about the strength of his hand, the responder must add his strength to that of the opener. The following guide offers a scale of strength for the responder:

Minimum hand: 6–9 points
Above-average hand: 10–12 points
Maximum hand: 13 or more points

BIDDING WHEN
Both Hands Are Minimum

Both hands are minimum when the opener has 13–16 points and the responder has 6–9 points. In this case, the responder will probably not bid to game. If opener and responder have found an eight-card or better fit in a suit, responder should pass. Pass would also be appropriate if opener has rebid **1 NO TRUMP**. Responder can rebid the suit he had originally bid at the 2 level with 8 or 9 points and a five-card suit. Responder can show his weak hand by bidding **1 NO TRUMP**.

BIDDING WHEN
Opener Has a Minimum Hand and Responder Has an Above-Average Hand

In this case, the opener has a minimum hand containing 13–16 points, but the responder has an above-average hand with 10–12 points. The responder can jump one level if he has a fit with the opener's suit. If he wants to make a forcing bid, the responder can bid a new suit but only at the 2 level.

Opener Has a Minimum Hand and Responder Has a Maximum Hand

Now, the opener has 13–16 points, but the responder has 13 or more points. The opener and the responder have both shown an opening hand. Two opening hands should enable the partnership to produce a game. If they have a fit in a major suit, responder should bid game. If no fit exists, the responder should bid **3 NO TRUMP** if he has stoppers in the unbid suits. If the fit is in a minor suit, the responder should have 15 or 16 points to bid game in the minor suit. If a **3 NO TRUMP** bid is inappropriate, the responder can jump to the 4 level in a minor suit. By previous partnership agreement, the opener can raise to game in the minor suit if he has some shortage points and his hand will be the dummy.

Opener Has an Above-Average Hand and Responder Has a Minimum Hand

When the opener has shown an above-average hand with 17–18 points and the responder has a minimum hand with 6–9 points, the responder must do some mathematics. With 17 or 18 points in one hand plus 6 or 7 points in the other hand, the total is less than the 26 needed to make a game. With 17 or 18 points in the opener's hand plus 8 or 9 in the responder's hand, the total of 25–27 points could produce a game. The options for the responder are therefore different depending on how many points are in his hand.

With 6 or 7 points, the responder should settle for a partial score and not bid game. If a fit exists or the bid is **2 NO TRUMP**, the responder should pass. Another possibility is for the responder to show four-card support of the opener's second suit or rebid the responder's own suit with a five-card suit.

With 8 or 9 points, the responder can jump to game with a fit in a major suit. He can also bid **3 NO TRUMP**. With some support in the unbid suits, the responder can also bid a new suit to force his partner to bid again. Showing support in an unbid suit can encourage the opener to bid in No Trump.

BIDDING WHEN
Both Hands Are Above-Average

If the opener has indicated 17–18 points and the responder has 10–12 points, the scenario requires a bid of game. The responder can bid game in a major suit where the partnership has a fit. A bid of **3 NO TRUMP** is a possibility with some support in the unbid suits. The responder can bid a new suit. This forcing bid indicates support in a suit and asks the opener to consider a bid of No Trump.

BIDDING WHEN
Opener Has an Above-Average Hand and
Responder Has a Maximum Hand

A partnership with 17–18 points in the opener's hand and 13 or more points in the responder's hand should bid game in a major suit, a minor suit, or No Trump.

The responder should consider slam if a fit exists and he has more than 13 points after counting shortage points.

Opener Has a Maximum Hand and Responder Has a Minimum Hand

When the opener has indicated a level of 19–21 points and the responder has 6–9 points, the bidding may already be at game level. The responder can therefore pass. If a fit exists, the responder can bid game in a major suit. With some support in unbid suits, the responder can bid **3 NO TRUMP**. If a No Trump bid is impossible and a fit exists in a minor suit, the responder should consider game in a minor suit. In this case, the responder can count shortage points when his hand will be the dummy.

Opener Has a Maximum Hand and Responder Has an Above-Average Hand

A total of 29–33 points are possible when the opener has 19–21 points and the responder has 10–12 points. The final bid should be at least a game in a minor suit, a major suit, or No Trump. A slam bid is a possibility especially if both hands are at the maximum range of points. The partnership can consider cue bids, Blackwood, or Key Card Blackwood. Another possibility is to bid a new suit. This is a forcing bid that requires partner to bid again. A cue bid is bidding a suit which contains an Ace. This is usually done after a fit has been established.

BIDDING WHEN
Both Hands Are Maximum

When the opener has 19–21 points and the responder has 13 or more points, the partnership may very well have a slam. The responder should bid a slam in a suit or No Trump. A grand slam is a possibility.

Setting the Contract

The responder's rebid usually sets the contract. In some cases, the responder's rebid still asks more questions. Bidding up the line is an example.

Consider the following bidding. The opener bids **1 CLUB**. The responder answers **1 DIAMOND**. The opener then bids **1 HEART**. Responder follows with **1 SPADE**. All those bids are forcing. Opener can now give much information in his next bid. A bid of **1 NO TRUMP** shows a minimum hand, a bid of **2 NO TRUMP** shows an above-average hand, or a bid of **3 NO TRUMP** shows a maximum hand. Another possible bidding answer by the opener would be **2 SPADES** to indicate a minimum hand, **3 SPADES** to show an above-average hand, or a bid of **4 SPADES** to show a maximum hand.

The responder in his second rebid can usually set the contract. Otherwise, the opener in his second rebid can often set the contract or make a cue bid, Blackwood, or Key Card Blackwood.

Summary

Rebids by Responder

Opener Has 13–16 Points (Minimum) and
Responder Has 6–9 Points (Minimum)

- Pass
- A suit already bid
- **1 NO TRUMP**
- A new suit at the 1 level

Opener Has 13–16 Points (Minimum) and
Responder Has 10–12 Points (Above-Average)

- Jump in a suit already mentioned
- **2 NO TRUMP**
- A new suit (forcing)

Opener Has 13–16 Points (Minimum) and
Responder Has 13 or More Points (Maximum)

- Game in a suit or No Trump
- A new suit at the 3 level

Opener Has 17–18 Points (Above-Average) and Responder
Has 6–9 Points (Minimum)

- A suit already bid at the 1 level
- Pass
- A new suit at the 1 level
- Game in a major suit or No Trump with 9 or 10 points

Opener Has 17–18 Points (Above-Average) and Responder
Has 10–12 Points (Above-Average)

- **3 NO TRUMP**
- Game in a suit
- A new suit (forcing bid)

Opener Has 17–18 Points (Above-Average) and Responder Has 13 Or More Points (Maximum)

- Game
- A new suit (forcing bid)
- Consider a slam bid with 15 or more points

Opener Has 19–21 Points (Maximum) and Responder Has 6–9 Points (Minimum)

- Game in a suit
- Game in No Trump
- A new suit (forcing bid)

Opener Has 19–21 Points (Maximum) and Responder Has 10–12 Points (Above-Average)

- Game in a suit
- Game in No Trump
- A new suit (forcing bid)
- Try for slam with 12 points

Opener Has 19–21 Points (Maximum) and Responder Has 13 or More Points (Maximum)

- Try for slam
- A new suit (forcing bid)

Quiz

In each of the following hands, you hold the indicated cards as the responder. The bidding has proceeded as noted. What is your rebid as responder?

1.

♠ 7 4
♥ J 7 5 4
♦ K Q 7
♣ A 9 8 3
OPENING BID: **1 HEART**
RESPONSE: **2 CLUBS**
OPENER'S REBID: **3 HEARTS**

2.

♠ Q 9 5
♥ K Q 10 9
♦ K 6 4 2
♣ 9 5
OPENING BID: **1 HEART**
RESPONSE: **3 HEARTS**
OPENER'S REBID: **4 HEARTS**

3.

♠ 10 8 6 2
♥ A 10 7 6 5
♦ Q J 6 3
♣ K 3
OPENING BID: **1 CLUB**
RESPONSE: **1 HEART**
OPENER'S REBID: **2 CLUBS**

4.

♠ J 6 4
♥ Q 7
♦ A Q 9 8 7
♣ J 10 6
OPENING BID: **1 CLUB**
RESPONSE: **1 DIAMOND**
OPENER'S REBID: **1 SPADE**

5.

♠ 9 8 5
♥ A K Q 5 2
♦ Q 7 5
♣ 9 5
OPENING BID: **1 CLUB**
RESPONSE: **1 HEART**
OPENER'S REBID: **1 SPADE**

Each of the following shows the two hands for a partnership: the opener and the partner or responder. What are the appropriate initial bids for each hand and the proper second bids for each hand?

6.

OPENER	RESPONDER
♠ A 10 7 6	♠ Q J 8 3
♥ A 6	♥ K J 5 3
♦ K Q 5 2	♦ A 9 8
♣ 9 6 4	♣ K 2

7.

RESPONDER	OPENER
♠ A 2	♠ K Q 7 4
♥ A 9 6 5	♥ K Q 7 3
♦ K 4 2	♦ J 10 9
♣ 9 5 4 3	♣ A 7

8.

OPENER	RESPONDER
♠ A K Q 6	♠ J 10 8 4
♥ J 10 9 8	♥ A 6 4
♦ 7 6	♦ Q 10 3 2
♣ Q J 6	♣ 8 7

9.

OPENER	RESPONDER
♠ J 7	♠ K Q 4 2
♥ K 9 4 3	♥ 10 8 7 6
♦ K Q 10 5	♦ 9 8 6
♣ A J 8	♣ K 7

10.

OPENER	RESPONDER
♠ A K 7 3	♠ Q J 6 2
♥ A 9 5 2	♥ K 6 4
♦ 7	♦ Q 5 4 2
♣ K J 6 2	♣ A 4

11.

OPENER	RESPONDER
♠ K Q 6 5	♠ A J 4 2
♥ A J 4	♥ K 10 6 2
♦ Q 8 6	♦ 9 4
♣ J 10	♣ 9 8 7

12.

OPENER	RESPONDER
♠ K 8	♠ Q J
♥ A K 8 6 2	♥ 9 7 5 3
♦ K Q 7 3	♦ A J 4 2
♣ Q 4	♣ J 10 2

13.

OPENER	RESPONDER
♠ Q J 7 2	♠ A K 8 5 4
♥ K 3	♥ A 6 2
♦ 7 5 3	♦ J 9 8
♣ A K 6 2	♣ 8 7

14.

OPENER	RESPONDER
♠ A K Q J 7 2	♠ 10 8 5 4
♥ J 6	♥ Q 10 8 4
♦ 9 7	♦ A 8 3
♣ A 9 8	♣ 7 4

15.

OPENER	RESPONDER
♠ A 5 2	♠ 8 7 4
♥ K 7	♥ A 10 9 2
♦ A Q J 7	♦ K 9 6 4
♣ K Q 10 6	♣ 7 4

Answers

1. Opener has an above-average hand, and responder has 11 points with 1 shortage points; rebid **4 HEARTS**.

2. Responder had bid a limit raise with 1 shortage point; pass.

3. Opener shows a minimum hand. Show your balanced hand by rebidding **2 NO TRUMP**. If opener has 16 points, he may bid **3 NO TRUMP**.

4. Show your above-average hand by rebidding **3 DIAMONDS**.

5. Show your above-average hand by rebidding **3 HEARTS**.

6. Opener bids **1 DIAMOND**, responder bids **1 HEART**, opener rebids **1 SPADE**, and responder rebids **4 SPADES**. Using bidding up the line, the partnership found a fit. The responder bids game because he holds a maximum hand.

7. The hand on the left must pass initially. The hand on the right becomes the Opener by bidding **1 DIAMOND**. The responder bids **1 HEART**. Opener

rebids **2 HEARTS**, and the responder rebids **3 HEARTS**. Bidding up the line finds a fit. Opener shows the fit, and the responder shows an above-average hand by bidding **3 HEARTS**. Opener is at the maximum level for his minimum hand and will subsequently bid **4 HEARTS**.

8. Opener bids **1 CLUB**, responder bids **1 DIAMOND**, opener rebids **1 HEART**, and responder rebids **1 SPADE**. Bidding up the line has found a fit. Opener will then bid **2 SPADES**. Since both hands are at minimum level, the responder should pass.

9. Opener bids **1 DIAMOND**, responder bids **1 HEART**, opener rebids **2 HEARTS**, and responder passes. Bidding up the line has found a fit. Since both hands are at minimum level, the bidding cannot proceed higher.

10. Opener bids **1 CLUB**, responder bids **1 DIAMOND**, opener rebids **1 HEART**, and responder rebids **1 SPADE**. Bidding up the line has found the fit in Spades. Opener using shortage points re-evaluates his hand and will subsequently jump to **3 SPADES**. Responder will bid **4 SPADES**.

11. Opener bids **1 DIAMOND**, responder bids **1 HEART**, opener rebids **1 SPADE**, and responder rebids **2 SPADES**. Bidding up the line found the fit. When responder limits his hand by rebidding **2 SPADES**, the opener must pass.

12. Opener bids **1 HEART**, responder bids **2 HEARTS**, opener rebids **3 HEARTS**, and responder rebids **4 HEARTS**.

13. Opener bids **1 CLUB**, responder bids **1 SPADE**, opener rebids **2 SPADES**, and responder rebids **4 SPADES**. Opener starts with a convenient minor suit bid. Responder bids his five-card major suit. This is a forcing bid. Opener shows a fit and a minimum hand. Responder re-evaluates his hand to 14 points with a shortage point and bids game.

14. Opener bids **1 SPADE**, responder bids **2 SPADES**, opener rebids **4 SPADES**, and responder passes. Opener's hand is not balanced. With 7 points including one shortage point, responder can bid **2 SPADES**. Opener takes a small gamble and bids **4 SPADES**.

15. Opener bids **1 DIAMOND**, responder bids **1 HEART**, opener rebids **3 NO TRUMP**, and responder passes. Opener bids a convenient minor suit. Responder bids his four-card major suit. Opener rebids game in No Trump. Note that opener's hand was too strong for **1 NO TRUMP** and too weak for **2 NO TRUMP**.

6
NO TRUMP BIDDING

OPENING A BID at **1 NO TRUMP** requires a balanced hand and 16–18 points in high cards. A balanced hand contains no voids, no singletons, and no more than one doubleton. Some partnerships bid No Trump using a 15–17 range or a 16–18 range. Adjusting the responses in this chapter to fit the system you and your partner prefer is easy. Certain partnerships also do not bid **1 NO TRUMP** with a hand that contains a five-card major suit. These are partnership agreements that are basic to any partnership.

This discussion will use the 16–18 point range and not allow a bid of **1 NO TRUMP** with a five-card major suit. The points must come from high cards.

Responding to **1 NO TRUMP**

Many hands will play better in a suit contract rather than No Trump. Two methods allow a partnership to find a fit in a major suit.

The Stayman Convention

The Stayman Convention is a system to determine if a fit of four cards of a suit exists. The first requirement to respond using Stayman is a hand that contains at least 8 points. The second requirement is 1 or 2 four-card major suits in the hand. The Stayman Convention is an example of the use of an artificial bid. If the responding hand to a bid of **1 NO TRUMP** contains a four-card major suit and at least 8 high card points, the bid is **2 CLUBS**— an artificial bid.

What is the reason for this artificial bid? If the responder has a four-card major suit, why not simply bid it? The primary reason behind the Stayman Convention and the Jacoby Transfer Convention described below is to have the stronger hand as the declarer. When the stronger hand becomes the dummy hand during play, the opposition sees the power of the partnership displayed on the table and can use it to their advantage.

The **2 CLUBS** bid by responder tells the opener that the responder has 1 or more four-card major suits and at least 8 points. Opener then will bid his four-card major suit at the 2 level. If opener does not have a four-card major suit, he bids **2 DIAMONDS**. This is another artificial bid. Responder's bid of **2 CLUBS** and opener's bid of **2 DIAMONDS** indicate nothing about the actual holdings of Diamonds and Clubs, but they give considerable information at the 2 level. Opener knows his partner has at least 8 points and a four-card major suit. Responder knows that the opener has a balanced hand with 16–18 points and whether he has a four-card major suit.

The Jacoby Transfer Convention

The only requirement to respond with the Jacoby Transfer Convention is to have a five-card or longer major suit. This means that responder can answer an opening bid of **1 NO TRUMP** with 0–7 points when he has a five-card or longer major suit.

What is the reasoning behind the Jacoby Transfer Convention? With 0–7 points, a responder's hand probably has little value to an opener's **1 NO TRUMP** bid. If the responder's hand does contain five trump cards, it may be of significant help to be successful in a contract of **2 HEARTS** or **2 SPADES**.

Jacoby Transfer is much simpler than Stayman. In using the convention, the responder is telling the opener he has a five-card major suit by bidding the suit below it at the 2 level. This is another artificial bid. If responder has five or more hearts, he bids **2 DIAMONDS**. If he has five or more Spades, he bids **2 HEARTS**. Opener then rebids responder's major suit. After opener's rebid, the partnership has much information. The next chapter will discuss the exact bidding strategy to reach a final contract.

Responding to 1 NO TRUMP
Without a Four or Longer Card Major Suit

If responder does not have a four-card or longer major suit and less than 7 points, he must pass. With 8 or 9 points, he bids **2 NO TRUMP**. With 10–14 points, responder bids **3 NO TRUMP**. If responder has 15 or more points, he bids **6 NO TRUMP** or uses the Gerber Convention described below to ask for Aces.

Responding by Bidding
3 DIAMONDS or 3 CLUBS

Some partnerships play that a jump to **3 CLUBS** or **3 DIAMONDS** by responder is a "drop dead" bid that opener would then pass. In these cases, responder has at least a six-card suit and little strength. With a strong minor suit, he will bid **3 NO TRUMP**. The determining factor for responder is an entry for playing the hand. Opener may only have two cards in the suit and have trouble setting up the suit during play if the contract is in No Trump.

Bidding Options for Responder

Consider all the possible responses mentioned above in another way. After an opening bid of **1 NO TRUMP** by the opener, the responder has numerous options.

Bid 2 CLUBS
This is the Stayman Convention. It is an artificial bid that tells the **1 NO TRUMP** opener that responder has at least 8 points and at least 1 four-card major suit. Opener then bids his major suit if he has one. Without a four-card major suit, he bids **2 DIAMONDS**.

Bid 2 DIAMONDS
This is a bid using the Jacoby Transfer Convention. It is another artificial bid by which responder indicates that he has five or more Hearts. Opener then bids **2 HEARTS**.

Bid 2 HEARTS
This is another bid using the Jacoby Transfer Convention. It is an artificial bid by which responder

indicates that he has five or more Spades. Opener then bids **2 SPADES.**

Bid 2 NO TRUMP

This bid tells the **1 NO TRUMP** opener that the responder does not have a four-card or longer major suit but does have 8 or 9 points.

Bid 3 NO TRUMP

This bid tells the **1 NO TRUMP** opener that the responder does not have a four-card or longer major suit but does have 10–14 points.

Bid 6 NO TRUMP

A bid of **6 NO TRUMP** tells the opener that the responder does not have a four-card or longer major suit but does have 15 or more points. The following chapter will discuss how to reach a final contract.

The Gerber Convention

The Gerber Convention is an artificial bid that the responder uses to ask the opener to indicate the number of Aces in his hand. To use the Gerber Convention, responder makes an artificial bid of **4 CLUBS.** The opener responds with **4 DIAMONDS** to show a hand with no Aces or four Aces, **4 HEARTS** to show a hand with one Ace, **4 SPADES** to show a hand with two Aces, and **4 NO TRUMP** to show a hand with three Aces.

The responder can next ask the opener to indicate the number of Kings in his hand by bidding **5 CLUBS.**

Responder shows no Kings by bidding **5 DIAMONDS**, one King by bidding **5 HEARTS**, two Kings by bidding **5 SPADES**, three Kings by bidding **5 NO TRUMP**, and four Kings by bidding **6 CLUBS**.

After an opener has bid **1 NO TRUMP**, the responder should not jump to **4 CLUBS** with the Gerber Convention without having 15 or more points. Do not use the Gerber Convention if other suits have been bid at any time. Only use the Gerber Convention in **1 NO TRUMP** contracts unless a previous partnership agreement has indicated otherwise.

Rebids by Opener

Opener's response to **2 CLUBS**
This is the Stayman Convention. Opener should rebid his major suit if he has one. Otherwise, bid **2 DIAMONDS**.

Opener's response to **2 DIAMONDS**
This is the Jacoby Transfer Convention. Opener should rebid **2 HEARTS**.

Opener's response to **2 HEARTS**
This is the Jacoby Transfer Convention. Opener should rebid **2 SPADES**.

Opener's response to **2 NO TRUMP**
With 16 points, the opener should pass. With 17 or 18 points, the opener should bid **3 NO TRUMP**.

Opener's response to **3 NO TRUMP** *or* **6 NO TRUMP**
The opener should pass these bids by responder.

Opener's response to 4 CLUBS

This is the Gerber Convention in which the responder is asking for Aces. As mentioned above, the opener responds with **4 DIAMONDS** to show a hand with no Aces or four Aces, **4 HEARTS** to show a hand with one Ace, **4 SPADES** to show a hand with two Aces, and **4 NO TRUMP** to show a hand with three Aces.

Summary

Initial No Trump Bid

Bid **1 NO TRUMP** with a balanced hand and 16–18 high card points. A balanced hand means no voids, no singletons, and no more than one doubleton.

Response To 1 NO TRUMP Bid

0–7 points:

• Pass without a five-card major suit.

• With a five-card major suit, use the Jacoby Transfer Convention by bidding the suit immediately below the five-card major suit.

8–9 points:

• With no four-card major suit, bid **2 NO TRUMP**.

• With 1 or 2 four-card major suits, use the Stayman Convention by bidding **2 CLUBS**.

• With a five-card major suit, use the Jacoby Transfer Convention by bidding the suit immediately below the five-card major suit.

10–14 points:

- With no four-card major, bid **3 NO TRUMP**.

- With 1 or 2 four-card major suits, use the Stayman Convention by bidding **2 CLUBS**.

- With a five-card major suit, use the Jacoby Transfer Convention by bidding the suit immediately below the five-card major suit.

15 or more points:

- With no four-card major, bid **6 NO TRUMP** or use the Gerber Convention by bidding 4 Clubs.

- With 1 or 2 four-card major suits, use the Stayman Convention by bidding **2 CLUBS**.

- With a five-card major suit, use the Jacoby Transfer Convention by bidding the suit immediately below the five-card major suit.

Rebids by Opener

- If responder uses the Jacoby Transfer Convention by bidding **2 DIAMONDS** or **2 HEARTS**, answer with **2 HEARTS** or **2 SPADES**, respectively.

- If responder uses the Stayman Convention by bidding **2 CLUBS**, opener should bid 2 in his four-card major suit. With two major suits, bid the best major suit. With no four-card major suit, bid **2 DIAMONDS**.

- If responder bids **2 NO TRUMP**, pass with 16 points but bid **3 NO TRUMP** with 17 or 18 points.

- If responder bids **3 NO TRUMP** or **6 NO TRUMP**, pass.

- If responder bids **4 CLUBS**, indicate the number of aces held by using the Gerber Convention.

Quiz

In each of the following hands, you hold the indicated cards as the opening bidder. How many points does your hand contain, and what is your opening bid?

1.
- ♠ J 10 9
- ♥ A 7 6
- ♦ K 8 7 2
- ♣ A K J

2.
- ♠ A Q 8 7
- ♥ K J
- ♦ A J 6 2
- ♣ K Q J

3.
- ♠ A Q
- ♥ K 9 8 7
- ♦ Q J 9 8 7
- ♣ A

4.
- ♠ Q 8
- ♥ A K Q 4
- ♦ K Q 7 6 5
- ♣ J 6

5.
- ♠ J 7 3
- ♥ A Q 9
- ♦ K Q 10 8 5
- ♣ A J

In each of the following hands, you hold the indicated cards as the responder. Your partner has opened with a bid of **1 NO TRUMP**. How many points does your hand contain, and how do you respond to the bid by your partner?

6.
- ♠ 6 5
- ♥ K Q J 4
- ♦ K 7 5 2
- ♣ A K 6

7.
- ♠ Q 8
- ♥ A 10 9
- ♦ J 3
- ♣ 10 9 8 6 5 3

8.
- ♠ A 9
- ♥ K 7 6
- ♦ Q J 9 8 5 4
- ♣ 10 2

9.
- ♠ K Q 6
- ♥ A Q 9 6 2
- ♦ K Q 6
- ♣ 9 2

10.
- ♠ A J 7 6 3 2
- ♥ A Q 9 5
- ♦ J 8
- ♣ 9

11.
- ♠ Q 8 6 3
- ♥ A K 5
- ♦ 9 6 3
- ♣ 8 6 4

12.
- ♠ Q J 8 7 6
- ♥ A Q 2
- ♦ 10 7 4 3 2
- ♣ K

13.
- ♠ Q 6
- ♥ 9 8 6
- ♦ Q 7 6 5 4
- ♣ 7 4 2

14.
- ♠ 9 3 2
- ♥ J 6 4
- ♦ 9
- ♣ J 9 6 4 3 2

15.
- ♠ K 9 6 4
- ♥ A Q 4 3 2
- ♦ 9
- ♣ J 7 4

16.
- ♠ A 10 7
- ♥ 7 6 4 2
- ♦ J 2
- ♣ Q J 8 3

17.
- ♠ K 6 5
- ♥ Q 10 7
- ♦ K 8 6 2
- ♣ 8 7 3

18.
♠ K 10 7 2
♥ K 9 7 3
♦ K 9 6 4 2
♣ A

19.
♠ Q J 4 3
♥ A 9 3
♦ 10 7 3
♣ K 4 3

20.
♠ 10 7 6 5 2
♥ 10
♦ J 5 4 3
♣ Q 9 4

21.
♠ 10 7 4
♥ J 10 7 5 4
♦ 4
♣ 9 8 3 2

22.
♠ A K J 9 5
♥ A 5
♦ K 10 6 4
♣ 4 3

23.
♠ K 10 9 7 5 4
♥ 4
♦ A J 9
♣ 10 3 2

24.
♠ K J 7 6 5
♥ A 3
♦ Q 6 3
♣ 10 7 3

25.
♠ J 10 9 6
♥ A 10 8
♦ A Q
♣ A 8 5 2

Answers

1. 16 points and a balanced hand; bid **1 NO TRUMP**.

2. 21 points and a balanced hand; bid **2 NO TRUMP**.

3. 17 points, but the singleton makes the hand unbalanced; bid **1 DIAMOND**.

4. 18 points, but the two doubletons make the hand unbalanced; bid **1 DIAMOND**.

5. 17 points and a balanced hand; bid **1 NO TRUMP**.

6. 16 points; bid **2 CLUBS** in the Stayman Convention and then jump to slam.

7. 7 points; pass. The bid is better in **1 NO TRUMP** than in **3 CLUBS**. Entries may help to set up the Clubs.

8. 10 points; bid **3 NO TRUMP** because the opener's hand of 16 points and your hand of 10 points total 26 points.

9. 16 points; bid **2 DIAMONDS** using the Jacoby Transfer Convention.

10. 12 points; bid **2 HEARTS** using the Jacoby Transfer Convention. After opener rebids **2 SPADES**, bid **6 SPADES**.

11. 9 points; bid **2 CLUBS** using the Stayman Convention.

12. 12 points; bid **2 HEARTS** using the Jacoby Transfer Convention.

13. 4 points; pass because you do not have a five-card major suit.

14. 4 points in Clubs; bid **3 CLUBS** because the hand has no value in No Trump.

15. 10 points; bid **2 CLUBS**. With a fit in a major suit, bid game or bid game in No Trump after a **2 DIAMOND** rebid.

16. 8 points; bid **2 CLUBS** using the Stayman Convention.

17. 8 points; bid **2 NO TRUMP** because you have no four- or five-card major suit.

18. 13 points; bid **2 CLUBS** using the Stayman Convention.

19. 10 points; bid **2 CLUBS** using the Stayman Convention.

20. 3 points; bid **2 HEARTS** using the Jacoby Transfer Convention and then pass for your next bid.

21. 1 point; bid **2 DIAMONDS** using the Jacoby Transfer Convention. Pass for your next bid.

22. 15 points; bid **2 HEARTS** using the Jacoby Transfer Convention. Try for a slam in a later bid.

23. 10 points plus 3 shortage points; bid **2 HEARTS** using the Jacoby Transfer Convention. Then bid **4 SPADES**.

24. 10 points; bid **2 HEARTS** using the Jacoby Transfer Convention.

25. 15 points; bid **2 CLUBS** using the Stayman Convention. Try for a slam in a later bid.

7

FINAL NO TRUMP CONTRACT

THE PREVIOUS CHAPTER focused on an opening bid of **1 NO TRUMP**, the response by a partner to that bid, and the subsequent rebid by the opener. This obviously is not the end of the bidding. What is the next bid by the responder?

With the bidding that has occurred at this point, both partners now know considerable information about the holdings in the two hands. The rebid by the responder is important to establish the final contract for the partnership. The rebid by the responder depends on the number of points in that hand.

Rebid by Responder with 0–7 Points

After the responder had originally bid his hand using the Jacoby Transfer Convention, he should pass for his rebid if he has 0–7 points.

Rebid by Responder with 8 or 9 Points

If responder had first bid Diamonds asking opener to transfer to **2 HEARTS**, responder would rebid **2 NO TRUMP** to show 8 or 9 points. If responder had bid Hearts and opener had transferred to Spades, responder would rebid **2 NO TRUMP**. All rebids by responder after the transfer are No Trump bids that tell opener the number of points responder has. The reasoning behind the No Trump rebids by responder is to offer the opener a choice. When responder starts the Jacoby Transfer Convention with a five-card suit and opener completes the transfer, the responder still does not know if the partnership has a fit in a major suit. Opener could have started with two cards in that suit. Alternately, he could have a fit but may want to play the hand in No Trump.

An exception occurs when responder has started with a six-card or longer major suit. If responder has six or more cards in a major suit, he and the opener will have a fit in that suit. Opener must have at least two cards in that suit for a balanced hand. Responder would therefore rebid 3 in the major suit after the transfer. Responder can also count shortage points because his hand is potentially the dummy hand.

If opener had rebid **2 DIAMONDS** after responder had made a Stayman Convention bid of **2 CLUBS**, responder would rebid **2 NO TRUMP**. With no fit in a major suit, the contract should be in No Trump. Responder's **2 NO TRUMP** bid pledges 8 or 9 points. The same procedure occurs if opener rebids a major suit that responder does not have. The responder should rebid **2 NO TRUMP** with 8 or 9 points. If opener's rebid shows a fit, the responder would bid the suit with the fit at the 3 level with 8 or 9 points. Opener with 16 points would pass both the **2 NO TRUMP** or the 3 level bid in the major because 16 plus 8 or 9 do not total 26. With 17 or 18 points, opener can bid game in his choice of No Trump or the major suit fit.

For a scenario where opener has 2 four-card major suits, bid the better one first. If responder rebids No Trump, opener then knows that responder had started with a suit not mentioned. He can then bid 3 in that suit with 16 points or 4 with 17 or 18 points.

Rebid by Responder with 10–14 Points

Responder knows that he and his partner have sufficient points for game. After opener answers the Jacoby Transfer Convention bid, the responder rebids **3 NO TRUMP** with a five-card major suit or game in the major suit with six or more cards.

If responder had bid using the Stayman Convention and opener had rebid Diamonds, the responder would bid **3 NO TRUMP** without a major fit. If opener had rebid responder's major suit, responder would rebid game in the major. After opener rebids the responder's major suit to indicate a fit, the responder can re-evaluate his hand using shortage points. He may then have sufficient points to bid a slam.

Rebid by Responder
with 16 or More Points

After the transfer in the Jacoby Transfer Convention bidding, the best method for responder to show the strength of his hand is by bidding No Trump. A bid of **2 NO TRUMP** shows 8 to 9 points, a bid of **3 NO TRUMP** shows 10–14 points, and a bid of **4 NO TRUMP** shows 16 points or more.

This **4 NO TRUMP** bid could cause confusion without a prior partnership agreement. In this case, it is a quantitative bid showing points. The bid is not the Blackwood Convention bid discussed in a later chapter. Without a previous partnership agreement, the next bid could spoil a slam bid. Responder still wants to allow the opener to place the contract. He cannot bid the major suit because he does not know whether opener has two or more cards in the transferred suit.

If responder had bid Stayman and opener had rebid Diamonds showing no fit, responder should rebid **6** or **7 NO TRUMP** with 16 or more points depending on how many points he has.

If a Stayman Convention bid shows a fit, responder should rebid at the 6 or 7 level in the suit with the fit or bid the Blackwood Convention to ask for Aces.

Summary

Responses by Responder in No Trump Bidding

0–7 points:
Pass.

8–9 points:
- If responder's first bid was Diamonds, opener would bid **2 HEARTS** and responder would bid **2 NO TRUMP**.

- If responder's first bid was Hearts, opener would bid **2 SPADES**. Responder would bid **2 NO TRUMP**. If responder started with a six-card major suit after the Jacoby Transfer bid, rebid at the 3 level in the major suit.

- If responder had first bid **2 CLUBS** and opener had rebid **2 DIAMONDS**, bid **2 NO TRUMP**.

- If opener rebids a major in which responder does not have a four-card major suit, bid **2 NO TRUMP**.

- If opener rebids a major suit in which responder has four cards, rebid the major at the 3 level.

- With no four-card or longer major suit, bid **2 NO TRUMP**.

10–14 points:
- If opener rebids Hearts after responder's Diamond bid or bids Spades after responder's Heart bid, rebid **3 NO TRUMP**. If responder has a six-card major suit, rebid at the 4 level in that suit.

- If opener rebids diamonds or a major suit in which responder does not have four cards after responder's bid of **2 CLUBS**, rebid **3 NO TRUMP**.

- If opener rebids a major suit in which responder has a four-card suit after responder's bid of **2 CLUBS**, bid at the 4 level in that suit.

16 or more points:
- When opener rebids Hearts or Spades after responder had bid Diamonds or Hearts, bid **4 NO TRUMP**. (This is not the Blackwood Convention but a quantitative bid.) If responder holds six cards in the major suit, bid at the 6 level in that suit.

- If responder had first bid **2 CLUBS**, opener had rebid **2 DIAMONDS** or a major suit that is not a fit with responder, rebid **6 NO TRUMP**.

- If responder had first bid **2 CLUBS** and opener had bid a major suit that indicated a fit, bid at the 6 level in that suit.

Quiz

In each of the following hands, you hold the indicated cards as the opening bidder. What is your rebid after your partner makes the indicated response to your opening bid?

1.

♠ J 7 3
♥ A Q 9
♦ K Q 10 8 5
♣ A J
OPENING BID: **1 NT**
RESPONSE: **2 CLUBS**

2.

♠ A Q 8 7
♥ K J
♦ A J 6 2
♣ K Q J
OPENING BID: **1 NT**
RESPONSE: **2 HEARTS**

3.

♠ J 7 3
♥ A Q 9
♦ K Q 10 8 5
♣ A J
OPENING BID: **1 NT**
RESPONSE: **2 NT**

4.

♠ A 4 3
♥ K 4 2
♦ Q J
♣ K Q J 9 8
OPENING BID: **1 NT**
RESPONSE: **2 DIAMONDS**

5.

♠ A 4 3
♥ K 4 2
♦ Q J
♣ K Q J 9 8
OPENING BID: **1 NT**
RESPONSE: **3 NT**

6.

♠ A K Q
♥ Q J 2
♦ 10 9 8 7 2
♣ K J
OPENING BID: **1 NT**
RESPONSE: **2 DIAMONDS**

7.

♠ A K Q
♥ Q J 2
♦ 10 9 8 7 2
♣ K J
OPENING BID: **1 NT**
RESPONSE: **2 NT**

8.

♠ Q 9 8 7
♥ K J
♦ A J 6 2
♣ K Q J
OPENING BID: **1 NT**
RESPONSE: **2 CLUBS**

9.

♠ K Q 8
♥ A K 7 3
♦ K 4 2
♣ J 6 3
OPENING BID: **1 NT**
RESPONSE: **2 CLUBS**

10.

♠ K Q 8
♥ A K 7 3
♦ K 4 2
♣ J 6 3
OPENING BID: **1 NT**
RESPONSE: **2 DIAMONDS**

In each of the following hands, you hold the indicated cards as the responder. Your partner has opened with a bid of **1 NO TRUMP**. You respond with the indicated bid. The opener makes the rebid shown. What is your rebid?

11.

♠ Q 9 6 4 3
♥ 8
♦ K 9 6
♣ 9 6 4 3
OPENING BID: **1 NT**
RESPONSE: **2 HEARTS**
OPENER'S REBID: **2 SPADES**

12.

♠ Q 8 6 3 2
♥ 5 3
♦ K Q 5 3
♣ J 8
OPENING BID: **1 NT**
RESPONSE: **2 HEARTS**
OPENER'S REBID: **2 SPADES**

13.

♠ A 3
♥ K J 7 6 5
♦ Q 6 3
♣ 10 7 3
OPENING BID: **1 NT**
RESPONSE: **2 DIAMONDS**
OPENER'S REBID: **2 HEARTS**

14.

♠ A 5
♥ A K J 9 5
♦ K 10 6 4
♣ 4 3
OPENING BID: **1 NT**
RESPONSE: **2 DIAMONDS**
OPENER'S REBID: **2 HEARTS**

15.

♠ K 10 9 7 5 4
♥ 4
♦ A J 9
♣ 10 3 2
OPENING BID: **1 NT**
RESPONSE: **2 HEARTS**
OPENER'S REBID: **2 SPADES**

16.

♠ A K 5 2
♥ Q 7 6
♦ 8 4
♣ 10 9 3 2
OPENING BID: **1 NT**
RESPONSE: **2 CLUBS**
OPENER'S REBID: **2 DIAMONDS**

17.

♠ A K 5 2
♥ Q 7 6
♦ 8 4
♣ 10 9 3 2

OPENING BID: **1 NT**
RESPONSE: **2 CLUBS**
OPENER'S REBID: **2 HEARTS**

18.

♠ A K 5 2
♥ Q 7 6
♦ 8 4
♣ 10 9 3 2

OPENING BID: **1 NT**
RESPONSE: **2 CLUBS**
OPENER'S REBID: **2 SPADES**

19.

♠ 4
♥ K Q 10 4
♦ A 8 7 5 2
♣ Q 7 4

OPENING BID: **1 NT**
RESPONSE: **2 CLUBS**
OPENER'S REBID: **2 DIAMONDS**

20.

♠ K 9 6 4
♥ A Q 4 3 2
♦ 9
♣ J 7 4

OPENING BID: **1 NT**
RESPONSE: **2 CLUBS**
OPENER'S REBID: **2 SPADES**

21.

♠ 4
♥ K Q 10 4
♦ A 8 7 5 2
♣ Q 7 4

OPENING BID: **1 NT**
RESPONSE: **2 CLUBS**
OPENER'S REBID: **2 HEARTS**

22.

♠ 6 5
♥ K Q J 4
♦ K 7 5 2
♣ A K 6

OPENING BID: **1 NT**
RESPONSE: **2 CLUBS**
OPENER'S REBID: **2 DIAMONDS**

23.

♠ 6 5
♥ K Q J 4
♦ K 7 5 2
♣ A K 6
OPENING BID: **1 NT**
RESPONSE: **2 CLUBS**
OPENER'S REBID: **2 SPADES**

24.

♠ 6 5
♥ K Q J 4
♦ K 7 5 2
♣ A K 6
OPENING BID: **1 NT**
RESPONSE: **2 CLUBS**
OPENER'S REBID: **2 HEARTS**

25.

♠ K 5
♥ K Q J
♦ K 7 5 2
♣ A K 6 3
OPENING BID: **1 NT**
RESPONSE: **4 CLUBS**
OPENER'S REBID: **4 SPADES**

26.

♠ K J 10 9 4
♥ A K 4
♦ 10 9 5
♣ 7 3
OPENING BID: **1 NT**
RESPONSE: **2 HEARTS**
OPENER'S REBID: **2 SPADES**

27.

♠ K 10 7 2
♥ K 9 7 3
♦ 9 8 4 2
♣ A
OPENING BID: **1 NT**
RESPONSE: **2 CLUBS**
OPENER'S REBID: **2 SPADES**

28.

♠ Q J 4 3
♥ K 9 3
♦ 10 7 3
♣ K 4 3
OPENING BID: **1 NT**
RESPONSE: **2 CLUBS**
OPENER'S REBID: **2 DIAMONDS**

29.

♠ Q 10 8 7 5
♥ A K 8 7 2
♦ 9 6
♣ 3
OPENING BID: **1 NT**
RESPONSE: **2 DIAMONDS**
OPENER'S REBID: **2 HEARTS**

30.

♠ K 3
♥ A 9 8 6 5
♦ 7 4 3
♣ J 9 2
OPENING BID: **1 NT**
RESPONSE: **2 DIAMONDS**
OPENER'S REBID: **2 HEARTS**

Each of the following shows the two hands for a partnership: the opener and the partner or responder. What are the appropriate initial bids for each hand?

31.

OPENER

♠ K 6 5
♥ A 9 7
♦ K Q J 10
♣ A 7 5

RESPONDER

♠ Q J 4
♥ 10 8 3
♦ 8 4 2
♣ Q 9 6 2

32.

OPENER

♠ K 6 5
♥ A 9 7
♦ K Q J 10
♣ A 7 5

RESPONDER

♠ Q J 4
♥ 10 8 3
♦ A 4 2
♣ Q 9 6 2

33.

OPENER

♠ K 6 5
♥ A 9 7
♦ K Q J 10
♣ A 7 5

RESPONDER

♠ A Q 4
♥ K 8 3
♦ 8 4 2
♣ Q 9 6 2

34.

OPENER	RESPONDER
♠ 6 5 3	♠ Q J 10 9 8 7
♥ K Q J	♥ 8 4 2
♦ K 7 5 2	♦ A J
♣ A K 6	♣ 5 4

35.

OPENER	RESPONDER
♠ 6 5 3	♠ Q J 10 9
♥ K Q J	♥ 8 4 2
♦ K 7 5 2	♦ A J
♣ A K 6	♣ 8 7 5 2

36.

OPENER	RESPONDER
♠ A K 5 3	♠ Q 10 7 2
♥ A 6 4 2	♥ K 8 3
♦ Q 5	♦ K 7 4
♣ K Q 5	♣ J 7 3

37.

OPENER	RESPONDER
♠ A K 5 3	♠ Q 9
♥ A 6 4 2	♥ K Q 9 5 3
♦ Q 5	♦ J 4 2
♣ K Q 5	♣ 10 8 7

38.

OPENER	RESPONDER
♠ A Q 5 2	♠ K 4 3
♥ K 8 7	♥ Q J 6 4
♦ K 10 3	♦ A 9 7
♣ A 9 6	♣ Q 8 5

39.

OPENER	RESPONDER
♠ Q 9 8	♠ J 6
♥ K J 4	♥ Q 10 9 8 7
♦ A J 6 2	♦ Q 9 4
♣ K Q J	♣ 10 9 8

40.

OPENER	RESPONDER
♠ A K Q	♠ J 10 9 8 7
♥ Q J	♥ K 7 4
♦ K Q J 8	♦ 9
♣ 10 9 8 7	♣ A 6 5 4

Answers

1. Responder has bid the Stayman Convention. Since you have no four-card major suit, bid **2 DIAMONDS**.

2. Responder has bid the Jacoby Transfer Convention. Bid **2 SPADES**.

3. Since you have 17 points, bid **3 NO TRUMP**.

4. Responder has bid the Jacoby Transfer Convention. Bid **2 HEARTS**.

5. Pass.

6. Responder has bid the Jacoby Transfer Convention. Bid **2 HEARTS**.

7. Pass with 16 points.

8. Responder has bid the Stayman Convention. Bid **2 SPADES**.

9. Responder has bid the Stayman Convention. Bid **2 HEARTS**.

10. Responder has bid the Jacoby Transfer Convention. Bid **2 HEARTS**.

11. Responder has bid the Jacoby Transfer Convention. Pass.

12. Responder has bid the Jacoby Transfer Convention. Show 8 points by bidding **2 NO TRUMP**.

13. Responder has bid the Jacoby Transfer Convention. Show 10 points by bidding **3 NO TRUMP**.

14. Responder has bid the Jacoby Transfer Convention. Show 15 points by bidding **4 NO TRUMP**.

15. Responder has bid the Jacoby Transfer Convention. Since you have six Spades, the partnership has a fit. Count your shortage points and bid **4 SPADES**.

16. Responder has bid the Stayman Convention. You have no fit and 9 points. Bid **2 NO TRUMP**.

17. Responder has bid the Stayman Convention. You have no fit and 9 points. Bid **2 NO TRUMP**.

18. Responder has bid the Stayman Convention. You have a fit. By counting your 1 shortage point, you can bid **4 SPADES**.

19. Responder has bid the Stayman Convention. You do not have a fit. Bid **3 NO TRUMP** with 11 points.

20. Responder has bid the Stayman Convention. You have a fit and 14 points. Bid **4 SPADES**.

21. Responder has bid the Stayman Convention. You have a fit and 14 points when you count 3 shortage points. Bid **4 HEARTS**.

22. Responder has bid the Stayman Convention. The hands have no fit, but you do have 16 points. Bid **6 NO TRUMP**.

23. Responder has bid the Stayman Convention. The hands have no fit, but you do have 16 points. Bid **6 NO TRUMP**.

24. Responder has bid the Stayman Convention. The hands have a fit. With 17 points, you can bid **6 HEARTS**.

25. Since the responder has 19 points, he bids using the Gerber Convention to ask for Aces. The opener shows two Aces. Responder rebids **6 NO TRUMP**. If opener had shown three Aces, the responder would have rebid **7 NO TRUMP**.

26. Responder has bid the Jacoby Transfer Convention. With 11 points, you bid **3 NO TRUMP** to show 10–14 points and a five-card major suit.

27. Responder has bid the Stayman Convention. Since you have at least 10 points, bid **4 SPADES**.

28. Responder has bid the Stayman Convention. Since you have no fit and 9 points, bid **2 NO TRUMP**.

29. Responder has bid the Jacoby Transfer Convention. Show your 13 points when counting shortages and 2 five-card major suits by jumping to **3 SPADES**.

30. Responder has bid the Jacoby Transfer Convention. Bid **2 NO TRUMP** to show your 8 or 9 points.

31. With 17 points, opener bids **1 NO TRUMP**. With only 5 points and no five-card major suit, pass.

32. With 17 points, opener bids **1 NO TRUMP**. With 9 points and no four- or five-card major suit, responder bids **2 NO TRUMP**. Opener can then rebid **3 NO TRUMP**. Responder passes.

33. Opener bids **1 NO TRUMP**. With 11 points and no four- or five-card major suit, responder bids **3 NO TRUMP**. Opener then passes.

34. Opener bids **1 NO TRUMP**. Responder uses the Jacoby Transfer Convention and bids **2 HEARTS**. Opener rebids **2 SPADES** to answer the convention. Responder notes the fit with his six-card Spade suit, counts his extra points for shortages, and bids **4 SPADES**.

35. With 16 points, opener bids **1 NO TRUMP**. With 8 points and a four-card major suit, responder bids **2 CLUBS**. Opener rebids **2 DIAMONDS** showing no four-card major suits. Responder rebids **2 NO TRUMP** to show 8 or 9 points and no fit. Opener then passes.

36. With 16 points, opener bids **1 NO TRUMP**. With 9 points, the responder bids **2 CLUBS** using the Stayman Convention. With 2 four-card major suits,

opener bids **2 HEARTS**. Responder shows no fit in Hearts by bidding **2 NO TRUMP**. Opener knows responder had opened with four Spades but with only 16 points, and rebids **3 SPADES**. Responder with a square hand passes. (A square hand means 3-3-3-4 distribution.)

37. With 18 points, opener bids **1 NO TRUMP**. With five Hearts, responder bids **2 DIAMONDS** using the Jacoby Transfer Convention. Opener bids **2 HEARTS**. Responder shows 8 or 9 points by bidding **2 NO TRUMP**. Since opener has a fit and 18 points, he bids **4 HEARTS**.

38. With 16 points, opener bids **1 NO TRUMP**. Responder bids **2 CLUBS** using the Stayman Convention. Opener rebids his four-card Spade suit. Responder shows his 12 points by bidding **3 NO TRUMP**. Opener passes.

39. With 17 points, opener bids **1 NO TRUMP**. With five Hearts, responder makes a Jacoby Transfer Convention bid of **2 DIAMONDS**. Opener bids **2 HEARTS**. With 5 points, responder passes.

40. With 18 points, opener bids **1 NO TRUMP**. Responder bids **2 HEARTS** using the Jacoby Transfer Convention. Opener bids **2 SPADES**. Responder shows his 8 points by bidding **2 NO TRUMP**. Since opener has 18 points and good Spades, he bids **4 SPADES**.

8
WEAK TWO BIDS

ALTHOUGH MANY PEOPLE may still consider an opening bid of 2 in a suit as strong, the modern approach is to open all strong hands containing 22 or more points with the artificial bid of **2 CLUBS**. This gives a partnership the widest latitude to find the best contract.

An artificial bid of **2 CLUBS** leaves the opening bids of **2 DIAMONDS**, **2 HEARTS**, and **2 SPADES** for other purposes. Some partnerships use a bid of **2 DIAMONDS** for the Flannary Convention discussed in a later chapter. If you do not play the Flannary Convention, the modern approach is to use **2 HEARTS**, **2 SPADES**, and **2 DIAMONDS** as a preemptive weak 2 bid. The weak 2 preemptive bid can be offensive or defensive like its older brother, the weak 3 preemptive bid.

Most players consider an opening bid of 3 in a suit as a preemptive or weak bid. Open this bid with a seven-card or longer suit and no more than 10 points. The bid is probably more defensive than offensive. It often prevents the opposition from reaching a game contract.

Two Examples of Weak Two Bids

Consider the following situation. Your partner has passed, and your right-hand opponent (RHO) has also passed. In the third position, your hand contains 6 points with a six-card Spade suit topped by the Jack and 10. Your left-hand opponent (LHO) obviously has an excellent hand. His side will undoubtedly find a contract at game. Imagine the damage you could inflict on their bidding if you opened **2 SPADES**! If you did happen to win the bid for **2 SPADES** and did not make the contract, you would at least have prevented your opponents from making a game. This is an example of using a weak 2 bid defensively.

Now, consider another situation. You are the dealer, and you have a hand containing 9 points with a six-card Heart suit topped by K and Q. You therefore open **2 HEARTS**. Your LHO passes. Your partner has a hand that has at least five tricks and contains 2 Hearts of a Jack and a low-value card. He bids **4 HEARTS**. That contract is usually successful. A good weak hand for bidding at the 2 level should take five tricks. This example shows a weak 2 bid that works offensively.

Position and Quality

When making weak 2 bids, the position of the bidder plays an important role in his bidding decision. When it is your turn to bid and nobody before you has bid, consider your position. If you are in the first (dealer), second, or fourth position, your hand must be stronger than if you are in the third position. Third position can be weaker because your partner and your RHO have both passed. Your bid can then be very defensive as noted above.

The quality of the suit itself is important. In first, second, and fourth positions, your suit should preferably have two honors and 5 points. Your hand should have no more than one outside Ace or King. You should not make a weak 2 bid if your hand also contains a four-card major suit. In first, second, and fourth positions, the hand should contain 8–11 points. In third position, it can have as few as 6 points.

The following examples of hands in any suit show the positions in which a weak 2 bid would be appropriate:

K	Q	10	8	5	2:	All positions
Q	J	10	9	7	4:	All positions
J	7	5	4	3	2:	Third position
A	K	J	9	8	4:	All positions
Q	9	5	4	3	2:	Third position
A	9	8	7	5	4:	All positions
A	Q	J	9	7	4:	All positions
K	8	7	6	4	2:	Third position
J	10	8	5	3	2:	Third position
K	J	10	9	7	3:	All positions

In the hands that are suitable only in the third position, the first and second positions have not bid. The third position can therefore think defensively.

In fourth position after three passes, the bidder can pass so the hand is passed out. In Duplicate Bridge, you may want to bid on a slightly weaker hand. Three passes usually mean that the points have very even distribution. If your other cards are good, you may want to bid on a weak six-card suit.

In bidding and responding to weak 2 bids, vulnerability is important. If your side is not vulnerable, you can bid and respond with weaker hands. This is especially true when your side is not vulnerable, but your opponents are vulnerable.

Responses to Weak Two Bids

The usual response to a weak bid of 2 is to pass. Some exceptions do exist. If responder feels that the contract can be made at the 3 level but not the 4 level, he can raise to the 3 level. This would place the opposition at a definite disadvantage because the bidding has encroached on their bidding space. This is especially true if the opponents are vulnerable and your side is not vulnerable.

The responder may have a very good six-card or better suit of his own. If he has a good hand, he may want to ask opener if a fit exists in his suit. Responder should then bid his suit at the 3 level if a fit exists.

A **2 NO TRUMP** bid asks a different question. This bid by responder asks the opener to name a feature. A feature usually is a suit containing an Ace, a King, or a Queen and Jack. Responder may be thinking of a No Trump contract and has concern about entries. The responder may also want to know if a second common suit exists so he can bid game.

Rebids by Opener

Opener would pass any rebid of his original suit or any game bid when he had initially made a weak 2 bid. If responder bids his own suit in answer to a weak 2 bid and opener has at least two cards in that suit, the opener raises that suit by one level. If responder does not have two cards to make a fit, he rebids his original suit.

When responder asks for a feature, opener obliges by bidding the suit containing the feature if he has such a suit. Without a suit containing a feature, he rebids his original suit.

Summary

Requirements for Weak Two Bids

- A six-card suit headed by two of the three top honors or 5 points in the suit.

- A total of 6–11 high card points.

- Only one Ace and no more than one outside King.

- With favorable vulnerability or in third position, the requirements may be slightly less. Do not make a weak bid of 2 with a good four-card major suit.

Responses to Weak Two Bids

- Raise partner's suit to make game or to continue the preemptive bidding.

- Bid **2 NO TRUMP** to ask for partner's feature: A, K, or Q and J in a suit.

- Bid your own suit to see if a trump fit exists.

Rebids by Opener

- Pass any raise in your suit.

- Pass any game bid by partner.

- When partner bids a new suit, raise his suit with normal trump support or rebid your suit.

- In response to a bid of **2 NO TRUMP**, bid your suit that contains a feature if you have one. Otherwise, rebid your suit.

Quiz

In each of the following hands, you hold the indicated cards in any position unless otherwise noted. What is your bid?

1.

♠ K J 10 8 5 4
♥ 4
♦ A 9 3
♣ 9 8 2

2.

♠ 9 7
♥ K 10 7 6 5 4
♦ 10 2
♣ K J 8

3.

♠ K 3
♥ 9 2
♦ A Q J 9 8 5
♣ 10 9 3

4.

♠ A Q J 9 8 5
♥ A J 2
♦ 9 7 4
♣ 3

5.

♠
♥ Q J 10 8 7 2
♦ K 10 9 6
♣ 7 4 3

6.

♠ A J 10 6 5 4 3
♥ 3
♦ 7 6 4
♣ 9 8

7.

♠ A 6
♥ J 10 9 6
♦ Q 10 9 8 5 4
♣ 4
THIRD POSITION

8.

♠ 9 3
♥ A K J 9 6 2
♦ K 9 2
♣ 4 3
THIRD POSITION

9.

♠ K Q J 9 6
♥ 3
♦ A 6 2
♣ 9 8 4 3

THIRD POSITION

10.

♠ J 10
♥ A 3
♦ 9 7 3
♣ K J 9 7 5 4

In each of the following hands, you hold the indicated cards as the responder. Your partner has opened with a bid of **2 HEARTS**. Vulnerability is indicated. What is your responding bid?

11.

♠ K 5 3 2
♥ 2
♦ A K Q 10
♣ J 10 3 2

VULNERABLE

12.

♠ 5
♥ 9 4 3 2
♦ 7 6 4 2
♣ A K 10 7 3

VULNERABLE

13.

♠ A K 3
♥ K 10 2
♦ A Q 4 3 2
♣ 3 2

BOTH SIDES VULNERABLE

14.

♠ K Q 10
♥ 7 3
♦ K Q 9 7
♣ K 4 3 2

BOTH SIDES VULNERABLE

15.

♠ A J 9 7 6 5
♥ 8
♦ A J 10 3
♣ K 4

NOBODY VULNERABLE

Each of the following shows the hands for a partnership: the opener and the partner or responder. Neither side is vulnerable. What are the appropriate bids for each hand?

16.

OPENER	RESPONDER
♠ 9 7	♠ A 8 7
♥ K 10 7 6 5 4	♥ 9 8 3 2
♦ 10 2	♦ A K 8 7
♣ K J 8	♣ Q 6

17.

OPENER	RESPONDER
♠ K J 10 8 5 4	♠ A 3
♥ 4	♥ A K 6 5
♦ A 9 3	♦ K 10 6 4
♣ 9 8 2	♣ 7 6 4

18.

OPENER	RESPONDER
♠ 9 8	♠ 4 3 2
♥ K J 10 7 6 5	♥ Q 4
♦ 10 2	♦ A K 9
♣ Q 10 6	♣ K J 9 5 2

19.

OPENER	RESPONDER
♠ A Q 9 7 3 2	♠ 4
♥ K 9 2	♥ A Q J 10 8 7
♦ J 2	♦ K 10 9
♣ 9 7	♣ K 3

20.

OPENER	RESPONDER
♠ 9 7	♠ A K 6 3
♥ K Q 9 8 7 3	♥ J 4
♦ 10 8	♦ K Q 8 5
♣ A 9 7	♣ K 10 2

Answers

1. The hand contains 8 points. Bid **2 SPADES** in all positions.

2. The hand contains 7 points. Bid **2 HEARTS** only in the third position.

3. The hand contains 10 points. Bid **2 DIAMONDS** in all positions if vulnerable. If not vulnerable or in third position, bid **1 DIAMOND**.

4. Bid **1 SPADE**.

5. The hand contains 6 points with a void. Bid **2 HEARTS**.

6. Bid **2 SPADES**.

7. Bid **2 DIAMONDS**; the four-card major suit is poor.

8. Bid **1 HEART**; count length.

9. Bid **2 SPADES**. You hold a good five-card suit. Bid for defensive reasons.

10. Pass. A bid of **2 CLUBS** would indicate 22 or more points.

11. Since you are vulnerable, you should pass.

12. Pass.

13. Bid **4 HEARTS**. You should have sufficient tricks for a game since a weak bid of 2 should be able to take five tricks.

14. Bid **2 NO TRUMP**. With a favorable feature, you may then consider **3 NO TRUMP** or **4 HEARTS** if partner rebids **3 HEARTS**.

15. Bid **2 SPADES** showing a six-card suit with a fairly good hand.

16. Since you are not vulnerable, open **2 HEARTS**. Responder would bid **2 NO TRUMP** asking for a feature. Opener would then rebid **3 CLUBS** to show a feature in that suit. Responder would next rebid **4 HEARTS**.

17. Open **2 SPADES**. Responder would bid **2 NO TRUMP** asking for a feature. Opener would rebid **3 DIAMONDS**, and responder would jump to **4 SPADES**.

18. This is a weak hand. Bid **2 HEARTS** if you are not vulnerable or are in the third position. Responder would pass or ask for a feature. Opener would deny a feature by rebidding **3 HEARTS**, and responder would pass.

19. Open **2 SPADES** in the first, second, or fourth positions if vulnerable. If not vulnerable or in the third position, bid **1 SPADE**. If opener opens

2 SPADES, responder would respond **3 HEARTS**. With a fit, opener would rebid **4 HEARTS**. If opener bids **1 SPADE**, responder would respond **2 HEARTS**. Opener would then rebid his six-card heart suit. Responder would rebid **3 HEARTS**, opener would then rebid **4 HEARTS**.

20. Open **2 HEARTS**. Responder should bid **2 NO TRUMP** to ask for a feature. Opener would rebid **3 CLUBS**. Responder would then choose between **3 NO TRUMP** or **4 HEARTS**.

9
STRONG BIDS

MODERN BRIDGE BIDDING uses only two bids to indicate a strong hand: **2 CLUBS** and **2 NO TRUMP**. The **2 NO TRUMP** bid requires a balanced hand of no singletons, no voids, and no more than one doubleton with 20 or 21 points. The bid of **2 CLUBS** simply requires 22 or more points.

Responding to a 2 NO TRUMP Bid

Responder knows that opener has at least 20 points. He also knows that it takes 26 points in the two hands of a partnership to make a game in a major suit or in No Trump. Responding to a bid of **2 NO TRUMP** uses the same rules for responding to a bid of **1 NO TRUMP** but adjusted to the higher number of points.

Jacoby Transfer Convention

If responder has a five-card major suit, he would bid the suit before it at the 3 level to ask opener for a transfer. When the opener then bids the responder's suit, the responder rebids as follows:

0–4 points:	Pass
5–9 points:	**3 NO TRUMP**
10 or more points:	**4 NO TRUMP**

The **4 NO TRUMP** bid above is not the Blackwood Convention. It is a quantitative bid.

Using the knowledge that responder has a five-card major suit and the number of points, the opener can then place the contract.

If responder had started with a six-card or longer suit with 5–9 points, he would bid game after the transfer. With 10 or more points, he should consider trying for a slam bid.

Stayman Convention

With 5 points or more and a four-card major suit, responder should bid **3 CLUBS**. Opener would either bid his major suit or **3 DIAMONDS** if he does not have a four-card major suit.

With 5–9 points, responder would then bid 4 in the major suit if a fit exists or bid **3 NO TRUMP** if no fit exists. With 10 or 11 points, responder would evaluate his distribution and decide whether to try a slam bid. If he has 12–15 points, responder should bid **6 NO TRUMP** with no fit or 6 in the suit that has a fit. With 16 or more points, responder should bid a grand slam.

Responding with No Four-Card or More Major Suit

With no four-card or higher major suit, responder should bid as follows:

0–4 points:	Pass
5–9 points:	**3 NO TRUMP**
10 or 11 points:	Consider a slam bid.
12–15 points:	**6 NO TRUMP**
16 or more points:	**7 NO TRUMP**

With a good hand and a possible slam, responder should strongly consider using the Gerber Convention to ask for aces. (See Chapter 6 for an explanation.)

Responding to a Bid of 2 CLUBS

Responder immediately knows opener has at least 22 points. He must keep the bidding open until reaching game. Opener can pass before reaching game, but the responder cannot pass before then.

Two methods are available to respond to a bid of **2 CLUBS**. The most common response is a **2 DIAMOND** bid. This response can have two meanings. It can mean, "Partner, I am very weak." It can also mean, "Partner, I want to wait to allow you to name your suit."

A big danger when responding to a **2 CLUB** bid is bidding the opener's suit. This means his hand would be the dummy allowing the opponents to see the strength of the partnership. Responder should therefore only bid a major suit with at least five cards and a strong hand.

If responder bids a suit and opener rebids No Trump, responder knows that opener has a balanced hand. Responder should bid **3 NO TRUMP** with a weak hand or try for slam with a hand containing 10 or more points.

When opener bids his suit, responder must tell the opener whether they have a fit. If a fit does exist, responder should bid the suit at game level or try for a slam with a strong hand. Without a fit, responder should bid his suit or No Trump.

Control Responses

When opener makes a bid of **2 CLUBS**, the chances of a slam bid are very high. Knowing this, the opener wants to know the location of the aces and kings. The control response is a great technique for this. In control responses, a King counts one point and an Ace counts two points. Responder answers the **2 CLUB** bid as follows:

0 or 1 point:	**2 DIAMONDS**
2 points:	**2 HEARTS**
3 points from 3 Kings or A, K in different suits:	**2 SPADES**
3 points from Ace and King in same suit:	**2 NO TRUMP**
4 points:	**3 CLUBS**

Summary

Bidding 2 NO TRUMP

- Need 20 to 21 points and a balanced hand.

Responding to 2 NO TRUMP

- Jacoby Transfer: With 0 or more points and a five-card major suit, bid the suit before the five-card major suit.

- Stayman Convention: With less than 5 points, pass. With a four-card major suit and at least 5 points, respond **3 CLUBS**.

- With no four- or five-card major suit:
  - 0–4 points: Pass.
  - 5–9 points: Respond **3 NO TRUMP**.
  - 10–11 points: Consider slam by bidding **4 CLUBS** (Gerber Convention) or bid **3 NO TRUMP**.
  - 12–15 points: Respond **6 NO TRUMP** or use the Gerber Convention.
  - 16 or more points: Respond **7 NO TRUMP**.

Rebids by Opener

- Complete a Jacoby transfer.

- After a bid of **3 CLUBS**, bid a four-card major suit if you have one or bid **3 DIAMONDS**.

- After a **3 NO TRUMP** bid, pass.

- After a bid of **4 CLUBS**, respond with the number of Aces.

- After a bid of **6** or **7 NO TRUMP**, pass.

Responding to an Opening Bid of 2 CLUBS

- A response of **2 DIAMONDS** shows weakness or a desire to wait for opener to name his suit.

- A response in a major suit indicates a five-card suit with at least 6 points.

- Note that responder must keep the bidding open until a game contract occurs.

- An Ace counts 2 points, and a King counts 1 point.

Respond as follows:

- 0 or 1 point: **2 DIAMONDS**

- 2 points: **2 HEARTS**

- 3 points: **2 SPADES** for 3 Kings or Ace and King in different suits

- 3 points: **2 NO TRUMP** with Ace and King in same suit

- 4 points: **3 CLUBS**.

Quiz

In each of the following hands, you hold the indicated cards as the opening bidder. How many points do the hands contain and what is the appropriate initial bid?

1.

♠ Q 10 8
♥ A K
♦ K Q 3
♣ A K 10 5 3

2.

♠ A K 3
♥ 9 6
♦ A Q J 7 6
♣ A Q 2

3.

♠ A 7 3
♥ A K 8 7 2
♦ K Q 7
♣ A J

4.

♠ A Q 9 7
♥ A K 2
♦ K J
♣ K J 9 7

5.

- ♠ K Q J 5
- ♥ A 9
- ♦ A Q 9 6 2
- ♣ K 7

In each of the following hands, you are the responder. Your partner has opened with a bid of **2 NO TRUMP**. How many points do you have in your hand and what is your bid?

6.

- ♠ K 9 8 6
- ♥ 4 3
- ♦ Q 10 5 3
- ♣ 7 4 2

7.

- ♠ 8 3 2
- ♥ 9 8 7 4 3
- ♦ Q 8 6
- ♣ Q 7

8.

- ♠ A J 8 7 5
- ♥ J 5 4 3
- ♦ 9
- ♣ 7 5 3

9.

- ♠ 4 3 2
- ♥ 10 5 4
- ♦ J 7 3
- ♣ K J 9 8

10.

- ♠ 9 6 3
- ♥ K Q 9 8 2
- ♦ 6 4
- ♣ K 10 7

11.

- ♠ 9 8 7 5 3
- ♥ 10 5 3
- ♦ Q 9 7 3
- ♣ 6

12.

♠ A 7 3
♥ J 9 7
♦ A 9 8 6
♣ 8 7 4

13.

♠ 10 8 5 3 2
♥ J 9
♦ 9 8 6
♣ K 7 5

14.

♠ Q 5 2
♥ 10 9 7
♦ Q J 8 7 4
♣ 10 4

15.

♠ K 4
♥ Q J 4
♦ A Q 8 7 4
♣ K Q

Each of the followings shows the hands for a partnership: the opener and the partner or responder. What are the appropriate initial bids for each hand?

16.

OPENER

♠ K 6
♥ K Q 9 6
♦ K Q 3
♣ A K J 6

RESPONDER

♠ A J 8 7 5
♥ J 5 4 3
♦ 9
♣ 7 5 3

17.

OPENER

♠ A 4
♥ K 10 4
♦ K J 3
♣ A K Q 8 6

RESPONDER

♠ 8 7 3
♥ A J 5
♦ 5 2
♣ 9 7 5 4 2

18.

OPENER	RESPONDER
♠ A K 10 7 6	♠ J 3 2
♥ A 2	♥ 9 8 7 4 3
♦ A J 5 4	♦ Q 8 6
♣ A 10	♣ Q 7

19.

OPENER	RESPONDER
♠ A J 6	♠ 9 8 7 5 3
♥ K 9 4 2	♥ 10 5 3
♦ A K 8 4	♦ Q 9 7 3
♣ A Q	♣ 6

20.

OPENER	RESPONDER
♠ A 10	♠ K Q 6
♥ A K 9	♥ Q 4 2
♦ J 9 6	♦ A K 9 4 2
♣ A K Q 8 6	♣ 10 9

In each of the following hands, you hold the indicated cards as the opening bidder. How many points do the hands contain and what is the appropriate initial bid?

21.

♠ A K 8 5
♥ K Q 9
♦ A Q7
♣ A J 4

22.

♠ A K Q 8 7
♥ 5
♦ K 9 7
♣ A K Q 5

23.

♠ A 4
♥ A K Q 9 8 7 3
♦ A 10 3
♣ 3

24.

♠ A J 8
♥ K Q J 10 4
♦ A K 3
♣ A 3

25.

♠ K Q
♥ K J 6 5 4
♦ K J 5 2
♣ A

In each of the following hands, you are the responder. Your partner has opened with a bid of **2 CLUBS**. How many points do you have in your hand and what is your bid?

26.

♠ Q J 7 4 3
♥ A 9 5
♦ Q 9 2
♣ 5 4

27.

♠ K 9 3
♥ 10 7 5 2
♦ 3
♣ A J 10 4 3

28.

♠ 9 8 6
♥ K 9 7 2
♦ 6 3
♣ J 8 5 3

29.

♠ 7 5
♥ 5 4
♦ A Q 9 8 4 2
♣ 9 4 3

30.

♠ K 8 5 3
♥ 9 8 5 4
♦ A J 3
♣ 4 2

In each of the following hands, you open with a bid of **2 CLUBS**. Your partner responds with **2 DIAMONDS**. What is your rebid?

31.

♠ A K 7 4
♥ K Q 10 9 6
♦ A K 8
♣ K 3

32.

♠ A 3
♥ A
♦ A Q J 9 8
♣ A Q J 8 4

33.

♠ A K J
♥ K J 9 6
♦ A K 8
♣ A 9 8

34.

♠ A K
♥ K J 9 6 4
♦ A K 8
♣ A 9 8

35.

♠ A K Q 5
♥ K Q J
♦ K J 10 3
♣ A Q

Each of the followings shows the hands for a partnership: the opener and the partner or responder. What are the appropriate bids for each hand?

36.

OPENER	RESPONDER
♠ K Q J	♠ 10 6 5 2
♥ K Q 8 6 3	♥ A
♦ A Q 5	♦ K 10 6
♣ A	♣ J 7 6 4 3

37.

OPENER	RESPONDER
♠ K	♠ A Q 7 5
♥ A K 7 4 3 2	♥ Q J 9 8 6 5
♦ A J 6	♦ 9 2
♣ K Q 8	♣ 3

38.

OPENER	RESPONDER
♠ A Q 9 2	♠ K J 10 8 7
♥ A Q 8 6	♥ K 10 5 3
♦ A	♦ 4 2
♣ A K 7 2	♣ 9 3

39.

OPENER	RESPONDER
♠ A	♠ K 9 8
♥ A K Q J 8 7 6 2	♥ 4
♦ A Q	♦ K 10 7 5
♣ Q 3	♣ K 9 5 4 2

40.

OPENER	RESPONDER
♠ 9	♠ Q J 10 7 2
♥ A K Q 10 9 7 2	♥ J 2
♦ K Q 3	♦ A 7 5
♣ A 2	♣ J 8 7

Answers

1. The hand contains 21 points and is balanced. Bid **2 NO TRUMP**.

2. The hand contains 20 points and is balanced. Bid **2 NO TRUMP**.

3. The hand contains 21 points. Bid **2 NO TRUMP**.

4. The hand contains 21 points and is balanced. Bid **2 NO TRUMP**.

5. The hand contains 19 points and is not balanced. Bid **1 DIAMOND**.

6. The hand contains 5 points and has a four-card major suit. Bid **3 CLUBS**.

7. The hand contains 4 points and has a five-card major suit. Bid **3 DIAMONDS** using the Jacoby Transfer Convention.

8. The hand contains 6 points and has two major suits. Bid **3 CLUBS** using the Stayman Convention.

9. The hand contains 5 points and has no four-card major suit. Bid **3 NO TRUMP**.

10. The hand contains 9 points and has a five-card major suit. Bid **3 DIAMONDS** using the Jacoby Transfer Convention.

11. The hand contains 2 points. Bid **3 HEARTS** using the Jacoby Transfer Convention and then pass.

12. The hand contains 9 points but has no four- or five-card major suit. Bid **3 NO TRUMP**.

13. The hand contains 4 points. Bid **3 HEARTS** using the Jacoby Transfer Convention. Then Pass.

14. The hand contains 5 points but has no four- or five- card major suit. Bid **3 NO TRUMP**.

15. The hand contains 17 points. Bid **4 CLUBS** to ask for Aces using the Gerber Convention or bid **7 NO TRUMP**.

16. With 21 points, opener bids **2 NO TRUMP**. With 6 points, responder bids **3 CLUBS**. Opener then rebids **3 HEARTS**. Responder bids **4 HEARTS**.

17. With 20 points, opener bids **2 NO TRUMP**. With 5 points, responder bids **3 NO TRUMP**.

18. With 21 points counting length and an unbalanced hand, opener bids **1 SPADE**. Responder has 6 points counting shortage points. He bids **2 SPADES**, and opener rebids **4 SPADES**.

19. With 21 points, opener bids **2 NO TRUMP**. Responder bids **3 HEARTS** using the Jacoby Transfer Convention. If opener bids **3 SPADES**, responder passes.

20. With 21 points, opener bids **2 NO TRUMP**. With 14 points, responder bids **4 CLUBS** using the Gerber Convention. Opener then rebids **4 NO TRUMP** showing three Aces. Responder rebids **5 CLUBS** to ask for kings. Opener rebids **5 SPADES** to show two Kings. Responder then rebids **7 NO TRUMP**.

21. The hand contains 23 points. Bid **2 CLUBS**

22. The hand contains 22 points counting length. Bid **2 CLUBS**.

23. The hand contains 23 points. You can count both length and shortages because the trump suit is obvious. Bid **2 CLUBS**.

24. The hand contains 23 points. Bid **2 CLUBS**.

25. The hand contains 18 points counting length. Bid **1 HEART**.

26. The hand contains 10 points and has a five-card major suit. Bid **2 SPADES**.

27. The hand contains 8 points. Bid **2 DIAMONDS**.

28. The hand contains 4 points. Bid **2 DIAMONDS**.

29. The hand contains 6 points. Bid **2 DIAMONDS**.

30. The hand contains 8 points. Bid **2 DIAMONDS**.

31. The hand contains 23 points. Rebid **2 HEARTS**.

32. The hand contains 24 points. Rebid **3 CLUBS**.

33. The hand contains 22 points. Rebid **2 NO TRUMP**.

34. The hand contains 23 points. Rebid **2 HEARTS**.

35. The hand contains 25 points. Rebid **2 NO TRUMP** and allow partner to show his points.

36. With 22 points, the opener should bid **2 CLUBS**. The responder would bid **2 DIAMONDS**. The opener would rebid **2 HEARTS**. The responder would rebid **2 SPADES**. The opener would then rebid **2 NO TRUMP**, and the responder would rebid **3 NO TRUMP**.

37. With 22 points, the opener should bid **2 CLUBS**. The responder would bid **2 HEARTS**. The opener would rebid **3 HEARTS**. The responder would bid **4 NO TRUMP** using the Blackwood Convention. The opener would show two Aces by bidding **5 HEARTS**. Responder would then bid **6 HEARTS**.

38. With 23 points, the opener should bid **2 CLUBS**. The responder would bid **2 SPADES**, and the opener would rebid **6 SPADES**.

39. With 26 points, the opener should bid **2 CLUBS**. The responder would bid **2 DIAMONDS**. The opener would rebid **2 HEARTS**. The responder would rebid **3 CLUBS**. The opener would rebid **3 HEARTS**. The responder would bid **4 DIAMONDS**, and the opener would then rebid **6 HEARTS**.

40. With 23 points counting both length and shortage, the opener should bid **2 CLUBS**. The responder would bid **2 SPADES**. The opener would rebid **3 HEARTS**. The responder would rebid **3 SPADES**. The opener would bid **4 HEARTS**, and the responder would then pass.

10

TAKEOUT DOUBLES AND OVERCALLS

FROM MANY BRIDGE HANDS used as examples in preceding chapters of this book, the reader might draw the conclusion that only his partnership holds good cards. Obviously, this is not always the case. Opponents can have good holdings too. This chapter will describe how to bid a hand after the opponents have made an opening bid.

The bidding in this chapter is interference bidding. The techniques are takeout doubles and overcalls. Most Bridge players use some form of these bids.

Takeout Doubles

Typically, a takeout double shows a minimum hand. It can also show a hand that is too strong for an overcall. A takeout double indicates that you have at least 1 four- or five-card major suit and some support in the unbid suits. The takeout double is when you double an initial bid by your opponents. When you double an opponent for takeout, you are trying to find a fit with your partner. You are especially looking for a fit in a major suit. Using only one bid, you can give considerable information to your partner without raising the level of bidding.

If you double a bid of **1 CLUB** or **1 DIAMOND**, your partner will expect that you have at least 13 points, some strength in the unbid suits, and at least 1 four-card major suit. If you double an opponent's bid of **1 HEART** or **1 SPADE**, your partner can expect at least 13 points, some support in the unbid suits, and a four-card holding in the major suit not bid by the opponents.

Doubling your opponents with excessive points in the suit they are bidding may not be wise. Those points may be useless. Many partnerships do not bid a takeout double when they have a five-card major suit. They will overcall instead. If you use a takeout double, your partner will not know whether you have 11 or 13 points. The knowledge that you have a five-card major suit may outweigh that fact.

If you have a very strong hand and a five-card major suit, you may elect to double because you can bid your suit at a higher level later. As a responder to your partner's double, you are forced to bid unless your right hand opponent (RHO) bids or you have a sufficient hand so you think you can set the original bidder. The partnership needs to agree beforehand whether a bid is for takeout or penalty. Many partnerships use the bid of **3 DIAMONDS** as the dividing line. This means that a double of a bid higher than 3 Diamonds is a penalty double.

A responder who has 10 points or more should bid at the 2 level. If he has at least 12 points, he can bid at the 3 level. The partner who made the takeout double bid needs to know the strength of the responder especially since the responder was forced to bid.

Overcalls

An overcall is a bid of any suit after the opponents have made a bid. Many Bridge players think a strong desire to bid is the only requirement for an overcall. This is not true. A partnership must have made an agreement beforehand regarding overcall bids.

One very standard agreement is to bid an overcall only if you hold a five-card suit. The person making the overcall should have a stronger hand if he bids at the 2 level.

Most partnerships use an overcall bid to indicate a five-card suit and 10–12 points. A bid for a hand containing a six-card suit might be a weak 2 bid. A jump overcall with most partnerships is preemptive.

Summary

Takeout Doubles

- Takeout doubles are bids after an opponent bids.

- Hand should contain 13 points but may be very strong.

- Hand should contain at least 1 four-card major suit.

- Partner must bid unless right-hand opponent bids.

- Responder should respond a four-card major suit if he has one or bid his best suit.

- Partner may pass if he believes he can set the opponent's bid.

- Responder should jump with 10 points if he can at the 2 level.

- Responder may jump to the 3 level with 12 points or more.

Overcalls

- Hand must contain at least 10 high card points.

- Hand must contain five or more cards in the suit bid.

- With six cards, overcaller may consider a weak 2 bid.

- Responder to an overcall knows what his partner holds and can respond accordingly.

Quiz

In each of the following hands, you hold the indicated cards. Your RHO has made the indicated bid. How many points does your hand contain and what is your appropriate bid?

1.

♠ K Q 9 8
♥ 3
♦ A 10 7 6
♣ K Q 4 2
RHO HAS BID **1 HEART**

2.

♠ A 6
♥ A Q 10 8 6
♦ 8 2
♣ A 9 5 2
RHO HAS BID **1 DIAMOND**

3.

♠ 3
♥ K Q 9 8
♦ A 10 7 6
♣ K Q 4 2
RHO HAS BID **1 HEART**

4.

♠ A 8 5 4
♥ A 9 7 2
♦ A 6 3
♣ Q 5
RHO HAS BID **1 CLUB**

5.

♠ A J 5
♥ A Q 7 2
♦ A Q 3
♣ 9 6 2
RHO HAS BID **1 CLUB**

6.

♠ A 6 2
♥ 9 7
♦ 8 3
♣ A K Q 8 6 2
RHO HAS BID **1 DIAMOND**

7.

♠ K Q 7 6
♥ 8
♦ K 10 4 3
♣ Q 9 7 4

RHO HAS BID **1 HEART**

8.

♠ K Q J 9 2
♥ K 6 3
♦ 5 2
♣ J 7 2

RHO HAS BID **1 DIAMOND**

9.

♠ K Q 10 8 7 6
♥ Q 8 6
♦ K 9 7
♣ 3

RHO HAS BID **1 DIAMOND**

10.

♠ A J 10 6 3
♥ 4 3
♦ K 6 3
♣ K Q 6

RHO HAS BID **1 CLUB**

For the following, East opens with the indicated bid. Your partner who is South doubles. West passes. You hold the following cards as North. How many points does your hand contain and how do you bid?

11.

EAST OPENS **1 CLUB**

♠ 8 7 4
♥ J 9 6 5 2
♦ 9 6 2
♣ 4 3

12.

♠ Q 7 4 3
♥ K J 9
♦ J 9 7 5 4
♣ 3

13.

EAST OPENS **1 HEART**

♠ 10 9 7 4
♥ Q 8 6
♦ K Q J 8
♣ K 3

14.

♠ K 10 7
♥ K Q J 6
♦ 8 4 2
♣ Q J 5

15.

EAST OPENS **1 SPADE**

- ♠ 7 2
- ♥ A 9 7 5 2
- ♦ A K 3
- ♣ J 5 2

Each of the following shows the hands for a partnership in the North and South positions. East opens the bidding with the indicated bid. How many points does South hold and what is the appropriate bid? Assume that West passes. How many points does North hold and what is the appropriate bid?

16.

SOUTH	NORTH
♠ A J 10 9 5	♠ 8 6 3 2
♥ A K 8 5	♥ Q J 7 2
♦	♦ A Q 7
♣ A 10 8 2	♣ 6 5

EAST OPENS WITH **1 DIAMOND**

17.

SOUTH	NORTH
♠ A Q 6 4	♠ K 8 4 3
♥ K 10 5 4 2	♥ Q 8 6 3
♦ A 5	♦ 7
♣ K 8	♣ J 7 6 2

EAST OPENS WITH **1 CLUB**

18.

SOUTH	NORTH
♠ K 9 2	♠ 10 8 6
♥ 9 7 6	♥ J 8 4
♦ A Q J 10 7	♦ 9 8 4
♣ Q 7	♣ K J 9 3

EAST OPENS WITH **1 SPADE**

19.

SOUTH	NORTH
♠ 9	♠ A K 6 5
♥ K Q 10 7 6	♥ J 9 8 4
♦ 9 4 2	♦ A 10 8 3
♣ K Q J 9	♣ 7

EAST OPENS WITH **1 DIAMOND**

20.

SOUTH	NORTH
♠ A K 8 3	♠ J 5
♥ A 9 5 3	♥ 8 6 2
♦ 10 4	♦ J 9 3
♣ A 4 2	♣ K 9 6 5 3

EAST OPENS WITH **1 DIAMOND**

Answers

1. The hand contains 14 points and a four-card Spade suit. **DOUBLE.**

2. The hand contains 15 points with a five-card major suit. Overcall **1 HEART.**

3. The hand contains 14 points but has too many points in Hearts. Pass and plan to set the opponents.

4. The hand contains 14 points. This is an excellent **DOUBLE** since the hand contains 2 four-card major suits.

5. The hand contains 17 points. **DOUBLE** as a strong bid. No Trump is not a possible bid because no Club stopper exists.

6. The hand contains 15 points. Overcall by bidding **2 CLUBS**. Plan to bid them again. Count length.

7. The hand contains 13 points. **DOUBLE**. Count shortage points because your hand should be the dummy in a suit bid.

8. The hand contains 11 points. Count length. Overcall **1 SPADE**.

9. The hand contains 10 high card points plus length. Bid **2 SPADES**. This jump overcall is preemptive—a weak 2 bid.

10. The hand contains 14 points. Overcall **1 SPADE**.

11. The hand contains 2 points. Bid **1 HEART**.

12. The hand contains 7 points. Bid **1 SPADE**.

13. The hand contains 11 points. This is a strong hand. Jump to **2 SPADES**.

14. The hand contains 12 points. Pass and plan to set the opponents.

15. The hand contains 13 points. Partner has shown 13 points and four Hearts. Bid **4 HEARTS**.

16. With 14 points, South should **DOUBLE**. North should bid **2 HEARTS**, and South should rebid **4 HEARTS**.

17. With 17 points, South should **DOUBLE**. North should bid **1 HEART**, and South should then rebid **3 HEARTS**. North bids **4 HEARTS**.

18. With 13 points, South should overcall **2 DIAMONDS**. North should pass.

19. With 10 points, South should overcall **1 HEART**. With 15 points counting shortages, North should bid **4 HEARTS**.

20. With 15 points, South should **DOUBLE**. North should bid **2 CLUBS**, and South should pass.

11
OTHER BIDDING CONVENTIONS

EARLIER CHAPTERS IN THIS BOOK covered common bidding conventions for the modern Bridge player. Although the techniques apply to many hands, occasionally a player will want to use a very specific bidding convention with his partner. This chapter therefore explains bids that apply in unique cases. The chapter differs from earlier chapters by omitting the summary and quiz sections.

Help Bids

Help bids are rare, but the author finds them valuable. Consider a hand where North has 17 points and a five-card Spade suit. He opens with **1 SPADE**. South has 8 points and three Spades. He therefore responds with **2 SPADES**. North wants to bid game, but he worries about his three small Diamond losers. He therefore bids **3** in the suit in which he requires help—**DIAMONDS**. If South has help in Diamonds, he bids **4 SPADES**. If he has no help, he bids **3 SPADES**. Help can be a void, a singleton, an Ace, or any two honor cards.

Blackwood Convention

The very common Blackwood Convention is a system to ask for Aces. When your partner bids **4 NO TRUMP**, he is asking you to tell him how many Aces you hold. A response to the Blackwood Convention of **5 CLUBS** indicates no Aces, **5 DIAMONDS** indicates one Ace, **5 HEARTS** indicates two Aces, and **5 SPADES** says three Aces.

If your partner wants to ask for Kings, he next bids **5 NO TRUMP**. You then bid Clubs with no Kings, Diamonds with one King, etc.

Key Card Blackwood Convention

This bid is similar to the Blackwood Convention except it uses the four Aces plus the King of trump as five key cards. If the bidding has not established the trump suit, the fifth card is the King of the last suit bid.

The initial bid in the Key Card Blackwood Convention is **4 NO TRUMP**. If the responder has none or three of the key cards, he bids Clubs. If he has one or four of the key cards, he bids Diamonds. If the responder has two key cards without the Queen of Trump, he should bid Hearts. If he has two key cards with the Queen of Trump, he bids Spades. In summary, the bidding is as follows:

- 0 or 3 key cards, bid Clubs.

- 1 or 4 key cards, bid Diamonds.

- 2 key cards without the Queen, bid Hearts.

- 2 key cards with the Queen, bid Spades.

This convention has two methods of asking for Kings so a partnership agreement is necessary beforehand. The first method is the following after a **5 NO TRUMP** bid:

- Bid the suit containing a King.

- With two Kings, bid the lower suit avoiding the King of Trump.

- With no Kings, bid the Trump suit.

In the second method, the response is exactly like the Blackwood Convention, but it counts the King of Trump. Key Card Blackwood gives a bidder many answers and keeps the bidding low in case he wishes to stop at the 5 level.

Reverse Drury Convention

This convention allows a player to determine whether a partner who had bid after two passes has a legitimate opening bid or has opened with less than the required opening hand.

If a partner opens with a bid in a major suit and you have 11 or 12 points or 10 points with support for his major suit, you might want to consider game. You must determine if your partner has a legitimate opening bid. A bid of **2 CLUBS** asks that question. The opener then responds with Diamonds if he had started bidding with a full opening hand. He responds in his suit if he had opened with less than a legitimate opening bid.

When the partnership has this information, it can determine at what level it wishes to compete. With a long legitimate Club suit, the responder would bid Clubs again at the 3 level.

Michaels Cue Bid

This convention is useful to indicate a two-suit hand. In response to an opening bid of **1 CLUB**, the responder bids **2 CLUBS** to show both five-card majors. After an opening bid of **1 DIAMOND**, responder bids **2 DIAMONDS** to indicate both majors. With an opening bid of **1 HEART**, a bid of **2 HEARTS** shows Spades and an undisclosed minor. After an opening bid of **1 SPADE**, a bid of **2 SPADES** indicates Hearts and an undisclosed minor.

The most common use is raising Clubs or Diamonds to show both major suits. The responder bids with his best major suit. The Michaels Cue Bid requires at least 10 points.

Flannary Convention

This is a system in which you can tell your partner that you have five Hearts and four Spades with 11–16 points. The convention requires that the opener bid **2 DIAMONDS**. Note that a partnership cannot use this bid and the weak bid of **2 DIAMONDS**. Agreement on choice of a convention for the bid of **2 DIAMONDS** is therefore necessary beforehand.

The reasoning for using this convention is that the opener wants to show both majors. If he opened with **1 HEART**, he could not rebid **2 SPADES** with 11–16 points. That would be a reverse for which he does not have sufficient points. With 17 or more points, he can open **1 HEART** and reverse to **2 SPADES**. Responder with 10 points and support for one major should jump to the 3 level. With 14 or more points, he should bid game.

Fishbein Convention

This convention offers a defense against an opening preemptive bid at the 3 level. If the opposition doubles, it is a penalty **DOUBLE**. If the opposition bids the next suit up, it is for takeout.

Consider these examples. The opener makes a **3 CLUB** preemptive bid. The defense doubles. This is a penalty **DOUBLE**. If the defense bids **3 DIAMONDS**, he is making a takeout bid. This requires support in both major suits and Diamonds. This convention often allows partnerships to find and make many game bids.

Unusual No Trump Convention

The Unusual No Trump bid is a direct overcall of **2 NO TRUMP** over a bid of 1 in a suit. It shows at least five cards in each of the lowest unbid suits:

Bidding **2 NO TRUMP** after an opening bid of **1 CLUB** shows five Diamonds and five Hearts.

Bidding **2 NO TRUMP** after an opening bid of **1 DIAMOND** shows five Clubs and five Hearts.

Bidding **2 NO TRUMP** after an opening bid of 1 in a major suit shows five Clubs and five Diamonds.